TO

FROM

OCCASION

THE Joshua CODE

52 Scripture Verses Every Believer Should Know

O. S. Hawkins

COUNTRYMAN®

A Division of Thomas Nelson Publishers

THOMAS NELSON

Since 1798

NASHVILLE   DALLAS   MEXICO CITY   RIO DE JANEIRO

TO SUSIE,
*whose outer beauty
is only exceeded
by her inner beauty.*

ALL MY LOVE . . . ALL MY LIFE.

Published in Nashville, Tennessee, by Thomas Nelson®. Thomas Nelson is a registered trademark of Thomas Nelson, Inc.

Cover design by Left Coast Design, Portland, Oregon. www.lcoast.com

Thomas Nelson, Inc., titles may be purchased in bulk for educational, business, fund-raising, or sales promotional use. For information, please e-mail SpecialMarkets@ThomasNelson.com.

ISBN-13: 978-1-4003-2070-7

Printed in China

13 14 15 16 [RRD] 7 6 5 4

www.thomasnelson.com

TABLE OF CONTENTS

INTRODUCTION

*R*ecently, while listening to our seven-year-old grand-child quote from memory an entire chapter of the book of Psalms, I realized how few adults give thought, much less are intentional, to the discipline of Scripture memorization. Do they know, for instance, what the Joshua Code is? It is found in Joshua 1:8: "This Book of the Law shall not depart from your mouth, but you shall meditate in it day and night, that you may observe to do according to all that is written in it. For then you will make your way prosperous, and then you will have good success." The Joshua Code is a challenge to keep God's Word in our mouths through memorization and to keep it in our hearts through meditation "day and night."

Many consistent Bible readers today seem to think it is the *volume* of Scripture they can devour daily that is most important. The fifty-two chapters in this volume are designed to lead readers on a year-long journey, spending a week on one particular Scripture, memorizing it, and meditating on it so that it is incarnated within and becomes a living part of our very being. The outlines in each chapter can also be used by the busy pastor or Bible teacher as a guide to challenge their hearers to a year of Scripture memorization and meditation on these fifty-two verses every believer should know.

My own life was dramatically transformed when, as a seventeen-year-old man, I came to know Christ as my own personal Savior and Lord. I could count on one hand the number of times I could recall being in a church service, and I did not even know Matthew, Mark, Luke, or John were books of the Bible. The first week of my Christian experience, someone handed me a slip of paper with 1 Corinthians 10:13 written on it and then, looking me squarely in the face, said, "You better memorize this because you will need it!" Thus began a journey of Scripture memorization that has served to lead me every day since. That verse says, "No temptation has overtaken you except such as is common to man; but God is faithful, who will not allow you to be tempted beyond what you are able, but with the temptation will also make the way of escape, that you may be able to bear it." Only God knows how many times across the years I have arrived at temptation's corner and this verse, hidden in my heart and mind, came out of my mouth and kept me on the right path.

Scripture memorization enables us to take God's Word with us anywhere and everywhere without carrying our Bibles. It enables us to receive the Word into our hearts, retain it in our minds, and recite it with our mouths that we might speak it with power. This is exactly what our Lord did during His days of temptation in the wilderness of Judea. With each temptation Satan brought Jesus' way in Matthew 4, Jesus answered with, "It is written . . ." The

Word received and retained in our hearts and minds overcomes temptations when recited with our mouths.

Scripture memorization begins when we seek to understand the passage we are about to memorize. This is why there is an outline of the passage's meaning accompanying every chapter in this volume. When memorizing Scripture, I have found it helpful to write it out in my own handwriting, phrase by phrase, on a small note card. I keep the card in my pocket throughout the week, and numerous times during each day—while at my desk, at a stoplight in the car, or on other such occasions—I simply review it until the first phrase is memorized, then the second, and so on. It is helpful for me to quote the entire verse from memory up to a hundred times in order to "seal it" in my heart and mind before going to another verse. Periodic review over the next few weeks is also essential.

Another important aspect of the Joshua Code is to "meditate in [Scripture] day and night." I sometimes wonder if fears of Eastern mysticism have robbed some Christians of the art of meditation. Webster's defines *meditate* as "to engage in contemplation or reflection, to focus one's thoughts on: to reflect or ponder over." Or, as the Bible says, "Meditate on these things" (Philippians 4:8). This is exactly what Mary, the young teenage virgin girl from Nazareth, did when she received the word that she was pregnant and when her child was born. She "kept all these things and pondered them in her heart" (Luke 2:19).

She meditated, "pondered," upon these things. The Greek word here for ponder is a compound word meaning "to stir together," just as a cook would put different ingredients into a pot, stir them, and simmer them together. This was the essence of the psalmist's plea in Psalm 19:14 when he said, "Let the words of my mouth and the meditation of my heart be acceptable in Your sight, O LORD, my strength and my Redeemer." One of the disciplines I have found helpful in meditation is to repeat the verse again and again, putting the inflection on a different word each time. It is amazing how much insight comes from this simple practice for the young and the seasoned believer alike. The early church father Augustine said, "God's Word is shallow enough not to drown the young, but deep enough that the greatest theologian will never touch the bottom."

Thus we begin on our journey to make the Joshua Code a daily part of our lives as we recover the beauty of Scripture memorization and meditation. Yes, "this Book of the Law shall not depart from your mouth, but you shall meditate in it day and night, that you may observe to do according to all that is written in it. For then you will make your way prosperous, and then you will have good success." I believe there are fifty-two verses every believer should know by memory. Let's begin this journey with the first verse of the Bible.

1 EVERYONE HAS A WORLDVIEW

In the beginning God created the heavens and the earth.

GENESIS 1:1

*E*veryone has a worldview. We all view life through some type of lens. Certain predisposed persuasions or seemingly benign biases do, in fact, determine how each of us views our world. Presently, the Western world is engaged in a huge confrontation between competing worldviews.

I spent my boyhood years in the 1950s, when the Judeo-Christian worldview was front and center in America. Our young men and women had just returned from the European Theatre or the South Pacific at the conclusion of World War II. They married their high school sweethearts and began what sociologists now call the baby boom. We were a thankful and grateful people. Church attendance was at an all-time high, and Bible readings were everyday occurrences in public schools. We viewed our world through a modern yet moral lens.

My teenage years were spent in the 1960s. The assassination of President John F. Kennedy ushered in that decade, and something happened to the psyche of America. We became more introspective. It began to be reflected in the music of the day. Peter, Paul, and Mary sang, "The answer, my friend, is blowing in the wind." Suddenly our introspection revealed that the simple answers we thought we held were now questioned. Our worldview began to subtly change. For many, the answers to life's questions that they thought they believed seemed to be "blowing in the wind."

Then came the 1970s, ushered in on the throes of Watergate, *Roe v. Wade*, and Vietnam. Society became more skeptical. Again, it was reflected in the music of the day. Billy Joel's big hit in those days was "Only the Good Die Young." Skepticism became the lens through which many in our culture began to view their world.

This was followed by a bit of a reprieve in the 1980s. Ronald Reagan brought new hope as he spoke about that "shining city on a hill." Then came the 1990s. The Berlin Wall fell; the Cold War came to a sudden conclusion. Next, the new millennium was ushered in on the heels of September 11, 2001, and the War on Terror was launched with a significant effect on the worldview of many.

Even though worldviews may change across the decades, there is a single constant that does not change. The simple fact is that one's worldview can be determined by one's response to the first four words of the Bible: "In the beginning God . . ." If we believe these four words, then we will view our world through the lens of Scripture that does not change. If we do not, then we will continue to view our world through the lens of culture that continually changes.

Perhaps there is no other verse under such constant abuse and ridicule as Genesis 1:1. It demands the answers to three important questions: When? Who? What?

WHEN? *"In the beginning"*

It should be noted that history does not begin in Genesis 1:1 but back before it, way back in the eternal councils of God. There we find three things: love, glory, and eternal life.

Before Genesis 1:1, there was love. In His high intercessory prayer, the Lord Jesus prayed, "Father, I desire that they also whom You gave Me may be with Me where I am, that they may behold My glory which You have given Me; for You loved Me before the foundation of the world" (John 17:24). Before the foundation of the world that is reported in Genesis 1:1, there was love.

Back in the eternal recesses of God, before the events of Genesis 1:1, there also existed glory. Earlier in that same prayer, Jesus had prayed, "Now, O Father, glorify Me together with Yourself, with the glory which I had with You before the world was" (John 17:5). Long before what we refer to as the "beginning," the glory of God existed.

There also existed the promise of eternal life back before

the "beginning." The apostle Paul, writing to Titus and inspired by the Holy Spirit Himself, penned it thus: "In hope of eternal life which God, who cannot lie, promised before time began" (Titus 1:2). Our hope of eternal life and its promise was there "before time began," before "the beginning."

One should not think of Genesis 1:1 as the beginning of everything, for "in the beginning was the Word, and the Word was with God, and the Word was God." So that there be no mistake about whom he spoke, the apostle John added, "And the Word became flesh and dwelt among us, and we beheld His glory, the glory as of the only begotten of the Father, full of grace and truth" (John 1:1, 14).

WHO? *"God"*

The Bible translates the Hebrew word *Elohim* here as *God*. The significance is that the word is in its plural form. It is a plural noun, thus hinting to us in the initial verse of Scripture that God is one pictured as three: Father, Son, and Holy Spirit. Interestingly, the verb *created*, which follows this noun, is in the singular form, seemingly making a mockery of grammar. Yet it should be singular in that He is the great Three in One. We see this truth revealed later in Genesis 1 when we read, "Let *Us* make man in *Our* image" (Genesis 1:26, emphasis added). And then the following verse reads, "So God created man in *His* own image" (v. 27, emphasis added).

The doctrine of the Trinity is one of the great mysteries of the Bible. Yet, beginning with this first verse, the idea of the Trinity is woven throughout the Scripture. It is often illustrated by its similarities to H_2O, two parts hydrogen and one part oxygen. We all know this to be water—a liquid. However, it can also be a solid (ice) or a vapor (steam). Yet, in all three manifestations, it is still the same in nature: H_2O. And so it is with God manifesting Himself in three persons.

WHAT? *"created the heavens and the earth"*

There is a huge difference between *creating* something and *making* something. Many of us have made things, but none of us has ever created anything from nothing. A cabinetmaker may make a beautiful cabinet out of wood. However, he is totally unable to create the wood itself. The Hebrew word from which we translate *created* in Genesis 1:1 carries with it the connotation that something is created out of nothing.

This physical universe was spoken into existence by God Himself. Is it possible that, in the entire vast expanse above us, the solar systems, the constellations, and the measureless space, all having billions of stars moving in clocklike precision, do so without a master Creator and Designer? Is it also possible that no one else among the billions of people presently on the planet has DNA or a thumbprint quite like yours? And is that kind of creativity and variety possible without Someone behind it all who sees you as indescribably valuable?

As you memorize Genesis 1:1 this week, meditate on the rich meaning of each of these sacred words and remember that those first four words of the Bible determine one's personal worldview. Yes, indeed, "In the beginning God!" Make these four words the lens through which you view your world.

2 THE MOST OFTEN QUOTED VERSE IN THE BIBLE

"For God so loved the world that He gave His only begotten Son, that whoever believes in Him should not perish but have everlasting life."

JOHN 3:16

*I*f we ever memorize a verse of Scripture, it will most likely be John 3:16. It is the verse most often heard in the simplicity and beauty of a little child's voice proudly reciting it from memory. It is the one verse showing up on large placards at football games and other major sporting events. Those signs are located where television cameras cannot avoid its message. This is the one verse that has been spoken by many older saints as they breathed their final breath. It is the entire gospel in a nutshell.

Angel Martinez, the late evangelist who had memorized the entire New Testament, referred to John 3:16 as salvation's formula and observed that it contained four very insightful truths. It is the gospel in one verse. It reveals to us salvation's cause, its cost, its condition, and its consequence.

SALVATION'S CAUSE
"For God so loved the world"

The motivating factor behind God's redemptive plan for every man and woman is His love for us. He not only loves us, He *so* loves us! Later, the apostle Paul sought to describe this love by speaking of its "breadth, and length, and depth, and height" (Ephesians 3:18 KJV), "God is love" (1 John 4:16), and this deep emotion is what brings about the possibility of our redemption; knowing Him in the intimate relationship of Father and child. God's love for you is the motivating cause of salvation. "For God *so* loved . . ."

SALVATION'S COST
"that He gave His only begotten Son"

Our salvation, the free pardoning of our sin, and the promise of abundant and eternal life in Christ did not come without cost. Freedom is never free; it is always bought with blood. From the early chapters of Genesis, there is a scarlet thread woven throughout the pages of Scripture revealing the blood atonement. It climaxes in the final and complete sacrifice for sin on a Roman cross outside the city gates of Jerusalem. Jesus not only spoke of His love for us, "but God demonstrates His own love toward us, in that while we were still sinners, Christ died for us" (Romans 5:8). Our salvation in Christ came at a great cost: God "gave His only begotten Son."

SALVATION'S CONDITION
"that whoever believes in Him"

Salvation is not spelled "d-o," but "d-o-n-e." Many people, however, think their own good works are the pathway to eternal life. Consequently, they do this or do that, or they don't do this or don't do that, all in order to earn salvation. But our salvation is done. It is already purchased for us with the blood of Christ on the cross. Our part is to believe, to transfer our trust from ourselves and our own efforts to His finished work on the cross of Calvary.

To believe does not mean to simply give intellectual assent to the claims of Christ. It means to transfer our trust to Him alone for our salvation. The most pointed question in the entire Bible is asked of the apostle Paul by a Philippian jailer: "What must I do to be saved?" (Acts 16:30). Paul's immediate reply follows in the next verse: "Believe on the Lord Jesus Christ, and you will be saved." I believe *in* George Washington, but I don't believe *on* him; I don't trust my life to him. Salvation's condition is through faith—and faith alone—in the finished work of the Lord Jesus Christ.

SALVATION'S CONSEQUENCE
"should not perish but have everlasting life"

What a consequence! What a promise! Those without Christ are perishing, but those in Christ have the eternal promise of "everlasting life." This comes not from our own human efforts, morals, or good deeds, but the promise is to those who realize that God's love reaches down to us, was made possible through the payment of Christ, and is received by grace through faith alone; believing in the Lord Jesus Christ.

An unknown, yet wise old sage once explained John 3:16 like this:

> *For God* . . . the greatest Lover
> *so loved* . . . the greatest degree
> *the world* . . . the greatest company
> *that He gave* . . . the greatest act
> *His only begotten Son* . . . the greatest gift
> *that whoever* . . . the greatest opportunity
> *believes* . . . the greatest simplicity
> *in Him* . . . the greatest attraction
> *should not perish* . . . the greatest promise
> *but* . . . the greatest difference
> *have* . . . the greatest certainty
> *everlasting life* . . . the greatest possession

As you memorize this old and oft-repeated verse this week, meditate on the fact that love is always something you do and remember that "God so loved the world that He gave." Yes, God knows you, loves you, and has a wonderful plan for your life.

3 AMAZING GRACE

For by grace you have been saved through faith,
and that not of yourselves; it is the gift of God.

EPHESIANS 2:8

*C*hristianity has always been cross-cultural. Its message transcends the various cultures of the world. Its roots were in a first-century Middle Eastern Jewish culture. Later it deeply impacted a sophisticated European culture. Then it continued to spread westward and became the basis of a New World culture. Today it is growing exponentially in an Eastern culture.

The modern church sometimes forgets that the Christian faith is not simply cross-cultural, but has always been countercultural as well. Western culture today is telling us in a thousand ways that there are many different roads that lead to eternal life. Many contend we are all going to the same place, just simply getting there by different paths. However, the Bible reminds us that "there is a way that seems right to a man, but its end is the way of death" (Proverbs 14:12). Salvation is entirely God's work, in God's way, and according to God's will.

SALVATION IS GOD'S WORK
"by grace you have been saved"

Where does our salvation have its origin? Many today believe it is the work of man, that one can merit good favor by one's own good deeds. But Christianity is counter-cultural. Salvation began way back in the eternal councils of God in eternity past. Earlier in this Ephesian letter, the apostle Paul said that God "chose us in Him before the foundation of the world, that we should be holy and without blame before Him in love" (1:4). Salvation is God's work.

Our salvation is "by grace" and not in response to any good works we may or may not have done. It is provided for us wholly because of His grace, His unmerited and undeserved favor. The Father did not send the Lord Jesus to die for our sin because we kept begging and pleading with Him to do so. It was by His grace alone. There is a difference between mercy and grace. Mercy is *not* getting what we do deserve; grace is getting what we do *not* deserve. No wonder we call it amazing!

SALVATION IS GOD'S WORK IN GOD'S WAY
"through faith . . . not of yourselves . . . the gift of God"

Whenever I read this verse, I find myself wanting to shout those words, "Through faith, and that not of yourselves;

it is the gift of God"! And, in the context, the following verse continues, "not of works, lest anyone should boast" (Ephesians 2:8–9). Scripture says our salvation is by grace and through faith; that is, by trusting in God alone. The Greek preposition preceding the word *faith* indicates that our faith is the channel through which our salvation flows from God to us. It is *through* faith. In Israel archaeologists have uncovered an ancient aqueduct through which the Romans brought their fresh water from the Carmel Mountains in the north down to the port city of Caesarea. It stands today as a reminder, a word picture, of how our own faith is the aqueduct through which the living water of God's saving grace flows to us.

Paul's repetition of this truth that salvation is "not of yourselves" and "not of works" emphasizes the point. Go to India today and the religion of the masses will reveal some followers pulling wagons with giant hooks in their backs, others lying on beds of nails, and still others plunging into the Ganges River. All of these things are being done in a feeble attempt to appease the Almighty. But it is "by grace . . . through faith, and that not of yourselves; it is the gift of God." Certain followers of Islam today rush out to die in jihad in hopes of being ushered immediately into heaven and being welcomed by dozens of virgins. In Latin America, one can find people during the Holy Days of Obligation crawling on their knees up rocky paths to the top of mountains to be nailed to crosses, all in their morbid search for penance. But it is "by grace . . . through faith . . . not of yourselves; it is the gift of God."

There are only two religions in our world: true religion and false religion. One is a religion of works while the other is freely obtained "by grace . . . through faith." No amount of human effort, good deeds, or giving of our resources can buy God's favor. And what amazes me is that God is freely offering this incredible gift, and we still have to encourage and exhort people to receive it. Salvation is God's work ("by grace") in God's way ("through faith").

SALVATION IS GOD'S WORK IN GOD'S WAY, ACCORDING TO GOD'S WILL

Ephesians 2:8–9 cannot stand alone without the context of verse 10: "For we are His workmanship, created in Christ Jesus for good works, which God prepared beforehand that we should walk in them." This is an awesome thought—"we are His workmanship." We actually get our English word *poem* from the Greek word translated "workmanship." You are God's special creation, His own work of art. He so fashioned and formed you that no one else has DNA like yours. You are unique to Him and indescribably valuable. You are His workmanship, His own special work of art.

The believer is a new creation. He is "created in Christ Jesus." Paul, in his letter to the Corinthians, addressed this very fact, saying, "If anyone is in Christ, he is a new creation; old things have passed away; behold, all things have become new" (2 Corinthians 5:17). Christians are not men and women who have been improved upon because they took on a new set of moral standards. They are new creations in Christ Jesus, His own special "poem." Thus, the Christian life is not simply a changed life but an exchanged life.

And all this was "prepared beforehand" by God Himself "that we should walk" with Him. Not only is this salvation His work done in His way, but it is also according to His will.

As you memorize this valuable verse this week, meditate on the fact that God has made a way out of no way for any and all who will come to Him by faith alone in His finished work of redemption. And it is all because of His amazing grace! Yes, salvation is God's work, in God's way, according to God's will.

4 A PSALM FOR THE AGES

The LORD is my shepherd;
I shall not want.

PSALM 23:1

*V*irtually every educated mind in the English-speaking world has heard the words of this psalm of King David. Some of our earliest recollections are associated with these poetic passages. It is as though it never grows old. In fact, often when we come before these lines, we continue to find new meaning. Like John 3:16, these words have been spoken by many a soldier under a star-filled sky, during a dark night in a foxhole on some faraway battlefield. These are the words that are formed by the lips of many dying on their beds of affliction. These words, like a lullaby for fear, have brought hope and peace to millions across the centuries.

Before David was ever a king, he was a shepherd boy in the fields of Bethlehem. Later in life, as he penned this shepherd's psalm, he reflected on those days with his sheep. Only a shepherd could have penned the depth of meaning we find in the six short verses that make up the Twenty-Third Psalm.

One should read slowly these first five words of the psalm: "The ... LORD ... is ... my ... shepherd." Those five words hold the key and form the foundation of the entire psalm. Once sealed in our own hearts, these words tell us much about our relationship with this good and great Shepherd.

HE IS PREEMINENT
"THE LORD is my shepherd"

The Scripture does not say, "*A* lord is my shepherd." It says, "*The* LORD is my shepherd." There is no other Lord. He has no peer. You speak of Washington, and I can speak of Lincoln. You speak of Beethoven, and I can speak of Handel. You speak of Alexander, and I can speak of Napoleon. But when it comes to Christ, He stands alone—without peers. There is only one Lord! The Hebrew word translated *Lord* here in Psalm 23 is *Yahweh*. The Jews regarded this name as so holy, and stood in such awe of it, that they would not even speak it publicly.

Only the records of heaven have recorded how many martyrs in the early church went to their deaths and laid down their lives because they insisted on the truth of these first two words in this psalm, *The Lord*. They would neither bow nor bend to profess Caesar as lord. They gave their lives because they were convinced there was only one Lord and His sweet name was Jesus. Our God is still preeminent. He is *the* one and only Lord.

HE IS PRESENT
"The Lord IS my shepherd"

Oh, the depth of meaning of this little two-letter word for us. This great and preeminent Lord is with me right now: "The Lord *is* my shepherd." This is not past tense. It does not say, "The Lord was my shepherd." It is not future tense. It does not say, "The Lord will be my shepherd." He is present—"The Lord *is* my shepherd." He is with us at this very moment to meet our present needs.

Earlier, on the backside of an Egyptian desert, God called Moses from a burning bush to become the great emancipator of His people. When Moses briefly balked at going back to Pharaoh, he asked God who he should say had sent him. God replied, "I AM WHO I AM . . . Thus you shall say . . . 'I AM has sent me to you'" (Exodus 3:14). Unlike the other world religions, we do not have a leader who has long since departed the scene or one who is still yet to come. He is the great "I AM," not the great "I WAS" or the great "I WILL BE." No wonder David said, "The Lord *is* my shepherd." David would reinforce this in the initial verse of Psalm 46 by saying, "God is our refuge and strength, a very present help in trouble."

HE IS PERSONAL

"The LORD is MY shepherd"

There is a huge difference in saying, "The LORD is *a* shepherd" and saying, "The LORD is *my* shepherd." What a difference comes to life's circumstances and situations with that little word *my*. We may hear of someone's child who is deathly sick, and we have compassion and feel sorrow. But what a difference it makes if it is *my* child. This is not just any shepherd about whom the psalmist speaks. This is *my* shepherd.

This small two-letter word is an awesome addition to the text. We are not simply insignificant specks of protoplasm in this vast array of solar systems. The fact that the God of this universe is concerned about me personally gives purpose and meaning to my short sojourn on this small planet hung in His vast expanse. Oh, the thought of it! He is *my* shepherd!

Unfortunately, however, not everyone can say this. Our faith in Jesus must be personal in order to know Him. Those who have placed their trust in Christ know Him with the intimacy of Father and child, of Shepherd and sheep. Jesus said it thus: "My sheep hear My voice, and I know them, and they follow Me. And I give them eternal life, and they shall never perish; neither shall anyone snatch them out of My hand" (John 10:27–28). Christ's sheep know His voice, and they follow Him. He is personal. He is *my* shepherd.

HE IS PROTECTIVE
"The LORD is my SHEPHERD"

One thousand years after King David penned these words, there stood One who said, "I am the good shepherd. The good shepherd gives His life for the sheep" (John 10:11). When we read Psalm 23, we are reading about this great Shepherd-Savior.

Our Shepherd is protective. This is the very nature of a shepherd. Without a good shepherd, the sheep could not find their way to water or to other of life's necessities. The shepherd keeps a constant vigil for wild animals or other dangers that might harm his sheep. A good shepherd goes after the sheep that stray from the fold. Could one ever forget the story Jesus told of the lost sheep in Luke 15? Without a shepherd, sheep are virtually helpless. They cannot find their way through treacherous mountain passes or run fast enough to escape a predator, nor are they strong enough to defend themselves. In fact, sheep are not prepared for flight or fight. Just as sheep need a shepherd, so do we have need of our Shepherd. Yes, "the LORD is my *shepherd*."

A final thought: if you have ever observed a shepherd with his sheep, you have made an insightful observation. The shepherd is always out in front of the sheep; the shepherd is never behind them. Shepherds lead sheep; they do not drive them as cattlemen do their cattle. The shepherd leads, and the sheep follow. Our Lord will never force us or drive us against our will. However, He will lead us. All we have to do is follow. We can trust the One who has given His life for His sheep.

It might be that you will want to memorize all six verses of Psalm 23 this week. And, as you do, meditate on the fact that our great God is preeminent, present, personal, and protective. Yes, "the . . . LORD . . . is . . . my . . . shepherd."

5 THE FAMILY SECRET

And we know that all things work together
for good to those who love God, to those
who are the called according to His purpose.

ROMANS 8:28

＊＊＊＊＊＊＊＊＊＊＊＊＊＊＊

*A*nyone who has been raised in a family environment has his or her own share of family secrets. These little tidbits of reality are usually best kept within the small circle of family. For some, these family secrets are dark and hidden in the recesses of the mind. For most of us, these secrets are light, spontaneous, perhaps a bit embarrassing, and often downright funny.

Did you know that those of us who have been born into God's family also have a family secret? There is something that we know that those who are not part of God's forever family do not know. Our family secret is found in our verse for this week, Romans 8:28. On numerous occasions along my own Christian pilgrimage, I have climbed up on top of this verse and found refuge and hope in times of confusion or need. There are four factors related to "the family secret" that every believer should know.

THE FAMILY SECRET IS CONFIDENTIAL
"And WE know . . ."

Note carefully this plural pronoun *we*. Yes, *we* know. This verse is not intended to be understood by the world. To the lost person, these words are folly and even foolishness. They cannot be understood. Why? Because this is our family secret: "We know!" This verse only applies to true believers. Confront existentialists today who seem to see no real purpose in history; they have no hopeful explanation for sudden death, sickness, or various setbacks in life. The Christian comes along and says, "Yes, there is, but it is a family secret . . . '*and we know* that all things work together for good to those who love God, to those who are the called according to His purpose.'"

Interestingly, the Bible translates our English word *know* from a Greek word that means we don't even have to know experientially here. It is a stated fact; we just know intuitively. We have a family secret within God's family. It is confidential—but "we know!"

THE FAMILY SECRET IS CONSTRUCTIVE
"things work together for good"

This is one of the most comforting thoughts in all of Scripture: things that happen in life have a way of working together for our good. They are constructive. As we each look back over our Christian experience, how many events that we may have thought at the time were disastrous actually, in the end, worked out for good? Yes, "things work together" neither by accident nor blind chance. God Himself is behind the scenes in each of our lives.

One Greek word *synergia* translates this entire phrase in the language of the New Testament. We get our word *synergy* by transliterating this ancient word. There is a constructive and synergistic principle at work in our family secret. This certainly does not mean that everything that happens is good. In fact, many are confronted with things that are bad. There are financial failings, sicknesses, and disappointments ad infinitum. However, it does mean that God can take our mistakes and messes and work them together for our own good. King David realized this and recorded these poignant words for all posterity: "It is good for me that I have been afflicted, that I may learn Your statutes" (Psalm 119:71). As believers, we have a very special family secret that is confidential and constructive.

THE FAMILY SECRET IS COMPREHENSIVE
"ALL THINGS work together for good"

When I meditate on these words, I am prone to ask myself, "Can I really believe this?" Had the apostle Paul said "some things" or "many things" or even "most things" it would be a bit more palatable. But "all things"? *All things* may include unfair things. This was certainly true for Joseph who was sold into slavery and later falsely accused of a crime that landed him in an Egyptian prison. *All things* may include difficult things. This was certainly true of Paul who was shipwrecked at Malta, stoned at Lystra and left for dead, and beaten and berated across the years of his missionary journeys. He knew well, from firsthand experience, what the Holy Spirit led him to write when he penned these words of our family secret.

Yes, *all* things are what? *Working together.* For what? *Good.* For example, I would not like to sit down for a meal and eat a bowl of baking soda. In and of itself, baking soda is distasteful. Nor would I look forward to eating a nice serving of flour. However, put them together, add a few other ingredients, stir them up, put them in the oven, and they turn into biscuits. And I love biscuits! All things, not necessarily in and of themselves, but when worked together in the tapestry of the cross, come out for our good and for God's glory. This family secret is not only constructive, but it is comprehensive. Yes, *all* things are working together for our good at this very moment.

THE FAMILY SECRET IS CONDITIONAL
"to those who love God, to those who are the called according to His purpose"

An unofficial poll taken of Sunday-morning church attendees asked them to quote Romans 8:28. The majority of them left off the first phrase "And we know." They simply began with the phrase "all things work together for good." But, interestingly, they also left off the last phrase that states, "to those who love God, to those who are the called according to His purpose."

Our family secret is conditional. It is not a blanket, unconditional promise for everyone. It is for those who "love God." Those who do not love Him are generally resentful about certain things that come their way. Only those who love Him and sense that there is purpose in their lives can understand the deep truth of Romans 8:28 and say with Job, "Naked I came from my mother's womb, and naked shall I return there. The LORD gave, and the LORD has taken away; blessed be the name of the LORD" (Job 1:21).

Love is something we do. In the Bible, it is always equated with action. Jesus said, "If you love Me, keep My commandments" (John 14:15). John framed it by saying, "For this is the love of God, that we keep His commandments" (1 John 5:3). Thus, we come to the bottom-line questions: Do we love God? Do we sense that we are called according to His purpose for our lives? Loving God and abiding in His will—His purpose—is the condition by which the truth of this verse comes home to our hearts.

As you memorize Romans 8:28 this week, meditate on the deep reality that God is awake and aware of everything that comes our way. He has His own wonderful way of turning our bitterness into blessing. We have that family secret in God's forever family.

6   BEING COMES BEFORE DOING

*"Blessed are those who hunger and thirst for
righteousness, for they shall be filled."*

MATTHEW 5:6

The Lord began His famous Sermon on the Mount
with a series of verses that have come to be known as
the Beatitudes. Our verse for this week is planted squarely
in the middle of this section. All the Beatitudes coming
before it point to it, and all of the ones following it issue
out of it. It is important to understand what our Lord is
driving home here. These are the *Be*-attitudes and not the
Do-attitudes. Being comes before doing, for what we do is
always determined by who we are.

The Beatitudes are not a set of rules, such as the Ten
Commandments, by which we are to live. The Ten Commandments have to do with actions; the Beatitudes have
to do with attitudes. The Ten Commandments have to do
with conduct; the Beatitudes have to do with character.
Why is it so imperative that we believers incarnate these
Beatitudes into our very being? It is because our actions

flow from our attitudes and our conduct issues out of our character. Let's take a journey down this pathway toward the Spirit-controlled life.

THE PATHWAY TOWARD THE LIFE OF BLESSING *Matthew 5:3–5*

This pathway begins with the first beatitude: "Blessed are the poor in spirit, for theirs is the kingdom of heaven" (Matthew 5:3). There is no premium to be found in poverty here. Note these are the poor in *spirit*. That is, blessed are the ones who realize their total abject poverty, spiritually speaking, apart from the Lord Jesus Christ.

The next step along this pathway is found in the second beatitude: "Blessed are those who mourn, for they shall be comforted" (v. 4). It is not enough to simply realize that without Christ we are poverty stricken spiritually. Blessing emanates from the fact that we are burdened by it, grieved at our spiritual condition, and actually mourn over the fact. Isaiah got to this place and exclaimed, "Woe is me!" (Isaiah 6:5). Job said, "I abhor myself" (Job 42:6). Peter said, "Depart from me, for I am a sinful man, O Lord" (Luke 5:8).

The final step in this part of the pathway is found in the next beatitude: "Blessed are the meek, for they shall inherit the earth" (v. 5). The picture of this Greek word, that we translate into English as "meek," is of an animal that has been domesticated. For example, it is a wild stallion that is ridden and "broken" by a cowboy so that it begins to go, turn, or stop with a slight move of the bridle's reins. The stallion's will has been broken and submitted to the master's will. And so it is with believers who know something of the Spirit-controlled life. First, they realize that without Christ, they are poverty stricken spiritually. This brings a burden to their hearts, and they mourn over their spiritual neglect. This is followed by their coming under the control of their Master, such that their will is lost in their Master's will. Thus, we join Jesus in His Gethsemane plea: "Not My will, but Yours, be done" (Luke 22:42).

THE PASSAGEWAY INTO THE LIFE OF BLESSING *Matthew 5:6*

Now at the fourth beatitude, we arrive at the passageway into the life of blessing: "Blessed are those who hunger and thirst for righteousness, for they shall be filled" (Matthew 5:6). It is not those who are hungering and thirsting after happiness who are being satisfied. It is those who strive for the righteousness of Christ in their own lives. The real irony is that the satisfied ones are not those who have arrived at righteousness but those who "hunger and thirst" for it. There is a paradoxical principle in play here. The believer is one who is hungering and thirsting and at the same time being filled in the very process.

At my former church there was a large ministry for the homeless people of our city. As many as four hundred beds housed multitudes of men and women each night, and on some days many times more than that were fed hot meals. I noticed something about men who were truly hungry. I would watch them as they stood in line to enter the building. A hungry man is a humble man. Many a man stood in that line, perhaps a dirty ball cap rolled up in his hands, as he waited for a meal with his head bowed in humility. Jesus said, "Blessed are those who hunger and thirst for righteousness, for they shall be filled." Those being filled with God's best are those who are hungering and thirsting for the things of God with a humble spirit.

THE PROOFS ISSUING OUT OF THE LIFE OF BLESSING *Matthew 5:7–10*

The first three beatitudes show us the pathway, the middle one shows us the passageway, and the final beatitudes reveal the proof that a person is living the Spirit-controlled life. The first proof is found here: "Blessed are the merciful, for they shall obtain mercy" (Matthew 5:7). Having received mercy in our thirst for righteousness, our first reaction is to show mercy to those who are around us. Show me someone who is hungering for righteousness, and I will show you someone who is showing mercy. On the other hand, show me someone who has no mercy on others, and

I will show you someone who has not walked down the pathway to blessing, much less entered its passageway.

The next proof of a Spirit-controlled life is found in these words: "Blessed are the pure in heart, for they shall see God" (v. 8). It becomes as natural as water running downhill for the individual who is pursuing God to have a pure heart in motives and morals.

The third proof is found in the next beatitude: "Blessed are the peacemakers, for they shall be called sons of God" (v. 9). Note that Christ pronounces a blessing here on the "peacemakers," not the peace lovers. These peacemakers are the active promoters of unity among the family of God. And note that they are not made sons of God by this outward manifestation, but they are "called" sons of God. They are recognized by others as such. Show me someone who tries to sow seeds of discord, and I will show you someone who is not thirsting after the things of God. On the other hand, show me believers who are pursuing God's heart, and I will show you people living in love and unity with those around them.

As we meditate on these words of Christ, we should be asking ourselves, *Am I extending mercy even to those who may not be deserving? Is my heart pure? Am I a promoter of love and unity with those around me?*

Finally, Jesus said, "Blessed are those who are persecuted for righteousness' sake, for theirs is the kingdom of heaven" (Matthew 5:10). Show me someone who never encounters spiritual obstacles, and I will show you someone not hungry for the things of God. If we are not meeting the devil head-on from time to time, we are most likely going the same way he is headed! Often one of the proofs of the Spirit-controlled life is spiritual confrontation and even conflict "for righteousness' sake."

It is interesting to note that these Beatitudes begin in verse 3 and end in verse 10 with the same promise: "For theirs is the kingdom of heaven." Could this be God's subtle way of reminding us that "our citizenship is in heaven" (Philippians 3:20), that although we live and interact here in this physical realm, we are, in fact, members of another kingdom—one that lasts throughout the endless ages of eternity?

As you memorize this verse this week, meditate on the fact that God has a life of blessing for you and remember that *being* comes before *doing,* for what we do is always determined by who we are. Or, in the believer's case, *whose* we are! Yes! "Blessed are those who hunger and thirst for righteousness, for they shall be filled."

7 GOD'S REMEDY FOR MAN'S SIN

All we like sheep have gone astray;
We have turned, every one, to his own way;
And the LORD has laid on Him the iniquity of us all.

ISAIAH 53:6

In the early chapters of Genesis—when God took the skin of an innocent, sacrificial animal and covered the nakedness of Adam and Eve—the sun of God's redemptive revelation concerning Christ and the cross began to rise. Thus, the Old Testament shadows of the cross began to emerge. Among these shadows is the revealing encounter of Abraham's sacrifice of his son Isaac in Genesis 22. Here we see a clear picture of the coming substitutionary death of Christ in the ram that took Isaac's place on the altar of sacrifice. This rising sun continued its ascent as we arrive at Exodus 12 and are introduced to the revealing story of the Passover Lamb, a sacrifice without blemish and spot. The blood of this sacrifice provided two things for the ancient Israelites: deliverance from death and freedom from slavery. As the sun of this revelation continues to rise, it casts a perfect shadow of the coming Messiah when it arrives at Isaiah 53. This is one of the mountaintops of Scripture and the most perfect shadow, the most vivid and vibrant picture, of the Lord Jesus found in the Old Testament.

Recently, while meditating upon Isaiah 53:6, I was captured by the first phrase, "All we like sheep." This metaphorical expression is used repeatedly throughout Scripture. One can never come to understand the deep meaning of this passage without gleaning an insight as to how it is that we resemble these woolly creatures, so dependent upon their shepherd for their survival. There are several principles in play here that merit our inquiry.

SHEEP ARE DUMB

Think about it. Have you ever been to a circus? If so, you most likely saw an array of trained animals. Huge elephants can be trained to stand on their back legs atop tiny stools. Monkeys can be trained to ride bicycles around in a small circle. Lions can be trained to jump through rings of fire. But have you ever seen a trained sheep? No. Sheep are dumb; they cannot be trained to do anything. They tend to wander around and frequently become lost because they simply follow their appetite with their heads down.

It is no wonder the prophet says, "All we like sheep have gone astray." Most people are opinionated. They talk profusely about politics, sports, and the like. However, if you want to hear an unintelligent conversation from the mouths of semi-intelligent people, get them into a conversation about God's plan of redemption and His remedy for sin. How ignorant are so many when it comes to life's greatest subject! Yes, we are more like sheep than some of us might want to admit.

SHEEP ARE DIRECTIONLESS

Sheep tend to simply wander and meander aimlessly along the hillsides. They have no sense of direction. This is not true with other animals. When I was a boy, our family pet was a dog by the name of Penny. One day she followed several older boys in the neighborhood as they rode their bicycles to a lake over ten miles from our home. Late in the afternoon they returned . . . without her. More than three weeks later, while eating dinner in our home, I heard a familiar scratching on the back door. I opened the door, and to my surprise there was my little dog, somewhat mangy and thin, but home at last. Many animals have an inner instinct that enables them to find their way home from great distances. But not sheep. They are directionless.

Yes, "all we like sheep have gone astray." So many men and women go through life without any real sense of direction, void of any perceived purpose. Many simply exist and have never learned how to live because, like sheep, they have no sense of direction in life.

SHEEP ARE DEFENSELESS

Almost every animal has some type of defense mechanism. Rabbits can run. Cats can scratch. Dogs can bite. Porcupines can puncture. Bees can sting. Goats can butt. Skunks . . . well, you get the point. But sheep? They are defenseless. They are totally unprepared for fight or for flight. They cannot fight other animals, and they cannot outrun those who seek them for prey. They are virtually helpless.

The man without the Lord Jesus Christ is like a sheep. He is helpless to get to the fold himself. He is on his own against "the wiles of the devil" (Ephesians 6:11); ill equipped for fight or flight.

Since we find ourselves like sheep—dumb, directionless, and defenseless—and since "we have turned, every one, to his own way," God has come to our rescue. "And the LORD has laid on [Jesus] the iniquity of us all." There is no clearer explanation of what transpired on the cross of Calvary than in these words of Isaiah 53:6. On the cross the Lord Jesus took our sin in His own body, bearing the wrath of God's punishment that we deserved. He suffered the hurt, the humiliation of our sin, the agony and the death we deserved to die. He died our death so that we could live His life. He took our sin so that we could take His righteousness. Not only was His death on the cross voluntary, but it was vicarious. He died in my place and yours. What a Savior!

As you memorize this verse this week, meditate on the fact that "God demonstrates His own love toward us, in that while we were still sinners, Christ died for us" (Romans 5:8). God does not have simply *a* remedy; He has the *only* remedy for our sin. "All we like sheep have gone astray . . . we have turned, every one, to his own way . . . and the LORD has laid upon Him the iniquity of us all."

8 THREE LEVELS OF PRAYER

"Ask, and it will be given to you; seek, and you will find; knock, and it will be opened to you."

MATTHEW 7:7

***

*W*hile Scripture memorization and meditation are vital to a victorious Christian life, the same can be said for a vibrant and virtuous prayer life. God speaks to us through His Word, and we speak to Him through our prayers of praise, petition, and intercession. Without the Bible, prayer has no real direction. And without prayer, the Bible is less dynamic. Like ham and eggs, corned beef and cabbage, steak and potatoes, the Bible and prayer go hand in hand.

In the Sermon on the Mount, the Lord outlined three levels of prayer that should characterize the prayer life of each and every believer. In His words, we are to "ask . . . seek . . . knock." Effective prayer is wrapped up with His will for our lives. If we know His will in a matter, we "ask." If we do not know His will, we are to "seek." If we know His will but the answer has not come, we are to "knock" until the door opens. Many believers never rise above the first level of prayer to the level of seeking, much less to the level of knocking. Effective prayers are those that beseech the throne of grace on all three levels.

THE LEVEL OF PRESENTING A PETITION *"Ask, and it will be given to you"*

We must ask. Ironically, as simple as this may seem, some find it difficult. There are those who are too proud or too self-sufficient to ever ask anyone for anything. Thus, for them, asking God is something almost unthinkable.

In the language of the New Testament, the verbs *ask, seek,* and *find* are in their present active imperative form. This simply means that the subject is performing the action, the action is ongoing, and it is a command, not an option. Thus, Christ is saying here that we are to keep on asking, keep on seeking, and keep on knocking.

On this first level of prayer, intercessors ask and have the promise of God that they will "receive." When you know God's will in a matter, you can ask and have the confidence that you will receive. This is why when one prays to receive Christ, confident that it is the Lord's will that none should "perish" (John 3:16), this person receives the gift of eternal life. However, there are times when we have asked for certain things and did not receive them because they were contrary to God's will for us. Quite honestly, in retrospect across the years, I am thankful God did not give me all the things for which I sometimes selfishly asked Him.

THE LEVEL OF PRESSING A
PETITION *"seek, and you will find"*

There is a higher level of prayer than that of simply presenting your petition before God, and that is the level of pressing your petition. This is the prayer we pray when we do not know the will of God in a matter, and we seek until we find it. This is a deeper and more mature level of prayer because it puts self aside and is motivated by a deep desire to want to know the will of God in a matter. It involves an intense search for the heart of God coupled with a regular pattern of Bible reading. It is why the apostle Paul admonished us to "let the word of Christ dwell in you richly in all wisdom" (Colossians 3:16).

We are to keep on seeking with an intensity that goes far beyond the level of simply presenting our petitions. And the promise is that we will find God's perfect will for our lives if we don't give up. He does not want to veil His will from us; He desires that we know it and walk in it.

THE LEVEL OF PERSISTING WITH
A PETITION *"knock, and it will be opened to you"*

When we reach this higher level of prayer, it becomes readily apparent who is really serious and who is not. To keep on knocking requires tremendous perseverance (Luke 11:5–8). We pray on this level of persisting with a petition when we feel certain we know the will of God in a matter but have not seen it come to fruition as yet. We keep on asking . . . keep on seeking . . . keep on knocking and hold to the promise that "it will be opened to you."

There is a sense in which God deals with us as we do our own children. When they are small, we teach them to ask for certain things. Later, we teach them to seek after their desires. And, because we know what is best for them, we encourage them to show real earnestness until doors are opened for them. We would do our children a great injustice if we treated them when they were ten years old as we did when they were two, or if we treated them when they were eighteen as we did when they were ten. When our children are small, we teach them to ask for things. When they get older and progress in school, we teach them to seek for answers to their homework. And, by the time they get to be young adults, they had best know how to knock.

We pray on this higher level of prayer when we know the will of God in a matter, yet the door remains closed. We keep on knocking. We never give up because we hold to God's promise: "It *will* be opened to you."

There are times in our Christian experience when we ask God in prayer for certain things, and it seems He does not answer us. However, He always answers. Sometimes the answer is *direct*: we pray and almost immediately we see the answer we requested. Other times our request is *denied*: God answers, but in a way that denies our request because He knows what is best for us. There are also times when the answer is *delayed*: God seems to put us in a holding pattern, and the answer eventually comes according to His timetable instead of ours. And then there are answers that are *different* from what we expected. Just because He answers our prayers in a different manner than we anticipated does not mean our prayers are not answered.

As you memorize this verse this week, meditate on these three different levels of prayer—and don't simply ask, but seek. And, yes, keep on knocking. Never give up. We have His precious promises: "It will be given to you . . . you will find . . . it will be opened to you."

9 THE PROOF IS IN THE PUDDING

Do not be drunk with wine, in which is dissipation;
but be filled with the Spirit.

EPHESIANS 5:18

*T*he secret of the Christian life is not that it is a changed life but an *ex*changed life. It is not that we simply take on a few new sets of moral standards and attempt to change our attitudes and our activities. Instead, at the moment of conversion, we give God our old life, He puts it away, and He comes to live in us in the person of the Holy Spirit. God's promise to us is that He will abide there, never to leave us, filling us and empowering us for service.

Paul made a contrast here between being "drunk with wine" and being "filled with the Spirit." The former causes one to be out of control; the other enables one to be in control. One is counterproductive; the other is productive. One makes one powerless; the other empowers. One often brings sorrow; the other brings joy.

The admonition of our verse is a mandate, the command to "be filled with the Spirit." God does not leave this as an option for the believer. Think of how every verb has a number, a tense, a voice, and a mood. When this command to "be filled" is broken down, it is of interest to note that the number is plural. The tense is present; that is, continuous action is involved here. The voice is passive, which means the subject doesn't act; it is acted upon by some outside force. The mood is imperative. It is a command. Thus, properly translated, the Bible is saying, "All of us must always be being filled with the Holy Spirit."

How can we know that we are being filled with God's Spirit? Better still, how will others know? Some contend it is in the reception and use of certain gifts of the Spirit. However, Scripture teaches quite the opposite in the very context of this command. As the old adage says, "The proof is in the pudding." The three verses following reveal to us the evidence by which we can know that Ephesians 5:18 is fulfilled in our lives. Yes, the proof is in the pudding.

THERE IS INWARD EVIDENCE
"singing and making melody in your heart to the Lord"
(Ephesians 5:19)

The first evidence that we are being filled and led by God's Spirit is that we will have a song in our heart. This is the inward evidence. Buddhists may have their impressive temples, but they have no song in their hearts. Hindus may have their mantras, but there is no song in their hearts. Muslims may pride themselves in almsgiving and perceived morality, but where is the song?

Notice that the Bible says we are not making rhythm in our hearts. Rhythm generally appeals to the flesh. Nor does it say we are making harmony, which appeals to the soulish realm of our emotions. It is the melody that gives us the song and appeals to the inner Spirit. Like Paul and Silas in a Philippian jail at midnight, we can also have a song in our hearts regardless of our circumstances.

THERE IS UPWARD EVIDENCE
"giving thanks always for all things to God" (Ephesians 5:20)

Here is found an attitude of gratitude to God. The individual being filled with the Spirit continues in a spirit of giving thanks always and is thankful for all things at the same time. While we have the confidence personally that we are being filled through the inward evidence of a song in our hearts, God sees it in our continual attitude of thanksgiving for all things. That's the upward evidence.

THERE IS OUTWARD EVIDENCE
"submitting to one another in the fear of God"
(Ephesians 5:21)

There is finally outward evidence that manifests itself in our relationship with others. This element of submission does not involve any sense of a lack of superiority. It is what the apostle was driving at when he said we should "esteem others better than [ourselves]" (Philippians 2:3).

This was never more beautifully illustrated than in the Upper Room when our Lord Himself became the servant of all and washed His disciples' feet. The believers who are being controlled by God's Spirit within will have a song in their hearts, will be thankful always for all things, and will be submissive in dealings with others.

How can we be filled with the Spirit who lives in us through the new birth? Step 1 is to *confess*. We must come clean with God. First John 1:9 says, "If we confess our sins, He is faithful and just to forgive us our sins and to cleanse us from all unrighteousness." The next step is to *crown* Jesus the Lord of our life. Romans 14:9 says, "to this end Christ died and rose and lived again, that He might be Lord of both the dead and the living." Finally, we are to *claim* all of this by faith. Mark 11:24 says, "Therefore I say to you, whatever things you ask when you pray, believe that you receive them, and you will have them." Confess! Crown! Claim! And "be filled with the Spirit." Once you are, then the proof will be in the pudding.

As you memorize this verse this week, meditate on how much God longs to reign as Lord on the throne of your heart, to fill you with His own fullness, and to empower you to overcome and live a life of blessing. After all, if it is great to get a blessing, it is even better to *be* a blessing. Confess your sins afresh and anew to Him. Crown Him the Lord of your life. Remove yourself from the throne of your heart and welcome Him there. Then claim God's fullness by faith.

10 THE FRUIT OF THE SPIRIT

The fruit of the Spirit is love, joy, peace, longsuffering,
kindness, goodness, faithfulness, gentleness, self-control.

GALATIANS 5:22–23

*I*n our previous chapter we examined the filling of the Spirit. We now turn our attention to the fruit of the Spirit. Fruit is *the delectable product of that which is created by the inner life of the vine.* On the eve of the Crucifixion, the Lord Jesus put it thus: "Abide in Me, and I in you. As the branch cannot bear fruit of itself, unless it abides in the vine, neither can you, unless you abide in Me" (John 15:4). Earlier on a Galilean hillside, He had said, "By their fruits you will know them" (Matthew 7:20). The fruit we bear as believers is evidence of His abiding on the throne of our lives.

At first glance, there appears to be a grammatical error in this verse. Note carefully: "The fruit of the Spirit *is* love, joy, peace . . ." The truth is that the fruit of the Spirit is love. Love, period. The nine fruits listed here are a cluster describing the evidence of the life of Christ within us. The fruit is singular here because it is the outcropping of one's life within. The fruit represents what we *are* rather than what we *do*. Here we are reintroduced to the principle of being before doing. What we do is determined by who, or whose, we really are!

The fruit described in Galatians is a triad: three clusters with three fruits each. They are reflected in a countenance that is *obvious*, conduct that is *orderly*, and a character that is *obedient*.

A COUNTENANCE THAT IS OBVIOUS *"love, joy, peace"*

Certain individuals seem to have a countenance of love, joy, and peace. The word translated "love" here is *agape*, God's own love. This is the highest level of love, the kind that always seeks the other's highest good. It is the same word we found back in the John 3:16 statement that "God so loved the world." It is no coincidence that love is first on the list of nine pieces of fruit here. It is the fountain of all others. Everything good issues out of God's love.

Next comes joy. It is the inner joy of Christ that reveals itself through our very countenance. This is the joy spoken of by Christ to His disciples on His last night in their presence: "These things I have spoken to you, that My joy may remain in you, and that your joy may be full" (John 15:11). If ever there were an attribute deserving of a place next to love, it is joy.

Peace makes up this triad of characteristics that are obvious in the countenance of the Spirit-controlled believer. Inner peace is God's very special gift to us. Again, on the evening before His death on the cross, Jesus speaks these words: "Peace I leave with you, My peace I give to you; not as the world gives do I give to you. Let not your heart be troubled, neither let it be afraid" (John 14:27). When we are abiding in the Spirit, the natural outcome is love, joy, and peace. It becomes obvious in our very countenance.

A CONDUCT THAT IS ORDERLY
"longsuffering, kindness, goodness"

Longsuffering is synonymous with *patience*. This translates from a compound word in Greek meaning "far from anger." This type of conduct, which is virtually void of a spirit of retaliation, cannot be worked up. It is produced from within. In our fast-paced, self-seeking world, patience does not seem to be in high demand. Like all the others in this cluster of fruit, longsuffering arises from love. Love's greatest triumph is not always in what love does but—more often than not—in what love refrains from doing.

The conduct of one who is abiding in Christ is also characterized by kindness. This same Greek word appears in the Ephesian epistle: "that in the ages to come He might show the exceeding riches of His grace in His kindness toward us in Christ Jesus" (Ephesians 2:7). Since Christ shows His kindness to us and He abides within us, we are to pass this kindness on to others in a conduct that is orderly.

Paul then introduced the fruit of goodness. Jesus "went about doing good" (Acts 10:38). There is a genuine sense of goodness about those who are abiding in Christ and being controlled by His Spirit. This orderly conduct is seen in the lives of many who have come to Christ. Where once they may have been impatient, now they have supernatural patience. Where once they were self-centered, now they show kindness toward others. Where once they may have been self-seeking, now their actions are characterized by goodness.

A CHARACTER THAT IS OBEDIENT
"faithfulness, gentleness, self-control"

What better could be said of someone than that he or she is characterized by faithfulness to God! Jesus reminded us that "he who is faithful in what is least is faithful also in much" (Luke 16:10). When we live a life of faithfulness, there is something inherent about it that strengthens our own sense of self-worth.

Another fruit that issues out of the abiding life in Christ is gentleness. This is the same word we translate "meek" in Matthew 5:5. On the surface it sounds a bit weak. However, it is one of the strongest character traits that can exist. The word picture is of a stallion that has been domesticated.

Or, as the cowboys here in Texas would say, "The horse has been broken." Once it was a bucking bronco and now it has a gentleness about it. This Greek word speaks of power on a leash. It describes an animal that has come under the control of a master. Gentleness is the natural outflow of that life within.

Finally, we come to the last piece of fruit in our cluster—self-control. It is impossible to achieve the highest level of self-control apart from God's abiding Spirit within us. Self-control does not come by the outworking of mere fleshly energy and effort. Like all the rest of the fruit, self-control is the outcropping of the life of the Holy Spirit within us. When we come to know Christ as a personal Savior, the Father sends the Holy Spirit not only to seal us, indwell us, and fill us, but also to produce fruit through us.

As we memorize this verse this week, meditate on a few questions: What about my countenance? Do others see love, joy, and peace in me? What about my conduct? Are patience, kindness, and goodness charactcristic of who I am? What about my character? Do I exhibit faithfulness, gentleness, and self-control? The fruit of the Spirit is *love*! Allow Christ's love to reign and rule in you and through you today. Being comes before doing, for what we do is always determined by who we are.

11 GOD'S PHONE NUMBER

"Call to Me, and I will answer you, and show you great and mighty things, which you do not know."

JEREMIAH 33:3

$\mathcal{I}$n Jeremiah 33:3, we find one of the most amazing promises in the entire Bible. An old friend calls this God's phone number. The line is never busy. Your call never goes to voice mail. He always answers—and He answers in a way that far exceeds our most optimistic expectations (Ephesians 3:20).

Prayer is one of the awesome privileges of the Christian life. Jesus said, "My house shall be called a house of prayer" (Mark 11:17). Before it is to be called a house of Bible teaching, a house of evangelism, a house of discipleship, or a house of social action, His house is to be called a "house of prayer." It is also of interest to note that the disciples asked of Him, "Lord, teach us to pray" (Luke 11:1). They never asked Him to teach them to preach or to evangelize or to organize or to mobilize. The only thing recorded that these faithful followers requested was that they be taught to pray. They observed Him for three years. They saw the intensity and frequency of His own personal prayer life. They knew that if they could capture the essence of prayer, they would be well on their way to preaching or doing any of the other ministries needed to be performed.

As we dial up God's phone number today, let's join the disciples in this request: "Lord, teach us to pray."

WHAT IS PRAYER?

Does the art of prayer mean praying ancient prayers by rote or ritual? God said, "Call to Me." Prayer is two-way communication. It is not just one-sided. On the Emmaus Road the two disciples exclaimed, "Did not our heart burn within us while [Jesus] talked with us on the road, and while He opened the Scriptures to us?" (Luke 24:32). Burning hearts come when we hear from the Lord, and we hear from Him, as they did, when He opens the Scripture to us.

Prayer is the talking part of a relationship. To have a positive and productive relationship with our wives, husbands, children, parents, or whomever else, there must be verbal communication. An early sign that a relationship is going sour is a lack of communication. And yet some Christians think they can go for days, or even weeks, without communicating with God. Prayer is the talking part of our relationship with the Lord, and it is vital for our own spiritual growth.

WHY WE PRAY

We should pray because the Lord knows better than we do about what we really need. It is prayer that makes God real to us. Just as the Bible gives our prayer direction, prayer brings a new dynamic to our Bible reading: God speaks to us through His Word, and we speak to Him through prayer. Prayer is like a symphony: the Bible is the score, the Holy Spirit is the conductor, and we are the instruments. As we read God's Word, the Holy Spirit leads us in our prayer life, and we actually begin to pray the Scriptures for ourselves and for others.

Another reason we should pray is because Jesus prayed. Think about it. If He who never sinned saw the need to pray so often, how much more do we, sinful as we are, need to call upon Him? Prayer has a way of setting us free. "The LORD restored Job's losses when he prayed for his friends" (Job 42:10). We should also pray because of the multitude of prayer promises we find in the Scriptures, not the least of which is Jeremiah 33:3.

WHEN TO PRAY

The Bible encourages us to "pray without ceasing" (1 Thessalonians 5:17). That is, we should live our lives in a constant state of communion with God as we go about our work and witness. Our Lord prayed "a long while before daylight" (Mark 1:35). On occasion, He spent whole nights in prayer (Luke 6:12). He prayed before each great crisis of life as evidenced in His prayer at the tomb of Lazarus. He prayed after the great accomplishments of life, as seen after He fed the multitudes on the Galilean hillside. Gethsemane reminds us of how Jesus prayed before the great temptations of life. The busier our Lord's life became, the more He gave priority to His own prayer life.

HOW TO PRAY

The place to begin in prayer is with the prayer of confession (Isaiah 59:1–2; Psalm 66:18). There is a sense in which it is not so much what we pray as it is what we *are* when we pray. *Confess* means "to agree with God." Our sin is not something to be minimized because it may not be as bad as someone else's. Nor is it to be excused because everyone else is doing it. Nor is sin some little vice to be laughed off. Sin is so serious it necessitated the cross. In this initial part of our prayer experience, therefore, we should confess sins of the tongue, or things we have said. We should confess sins of action, or things we have done. We should confess sins of thought, or those ideas we have allowed to reside in our minds. We should also confess sins of omission, for to know to do right and not to do it is also sin, according to the Bible. We have the promise that "if we confess our sins, [God] is faithful and just to forgive us our sins and to cleanse us from all unrighteousness" (1 John 1:9).

Next, we progress to the prayer of thanksgiving. We are to "enter into His gates with thanksgiving, and into His courts with praise" (Psalm 100:4). Thanksgiving is the gate through which we enter the throne room of prayer. Here we thank God for material blessings, physical blessings, spiritual blessings, and certain people who are important to us. Thanksgiving has a liberating effect. In fact, it was when Jonah prayed "with the voice of thanksgiving" (Jonah 2:9) that the Lord delivered him from the belly of the fish.

The prayer of confession and the prayer of thanksgiving lead us to the prayer of praise. Now that we have entered the gates with thanksgiving, we step into "His courts with praise" (Psalm 100:4). We thank God for what He has done; we praise Him for who He is! In the prayer of praise, we remember the question of our Lord to Peter, "Do you love Me more than these?" (John 21:15). Here we tell God that we love Him. We praise Him for His great attributes—His goodness, patience, holiness, and mercy. It is helpful to repeat stanzas of praise hymns to Him at this level of prayer.

This brings us next to the prayer of intercession. Here we approach God's throne on behalf of others. This is the prayer for our individual family members, friends, political leaders both national and local, those who need Christ, and even those who may have spoken against us.

After the prayer of intercession, we move to the prayer of petition. Here we ask God for anything and everything

He may have put on our heart. Finally, we arrive at the prayer of communion. This is the prayer that goes beyond mere words; this is when, with an open Bible, we are still and listen to God. When I first dated my wife, we talked incessantly, both afraid one of us might think the other was boring if the conversation lulled. However, after a few months, we would sit on her parents' sofa for long periods without saying a word . . . but we were still communicating! And so it is with the prayer of communion. This is the prayer that goes beyond mere words.

As you memorize God's phone number, meditate on the reality that prayer is a vital part of Scripture memorization and meditation. The Bible and prayer are inseparable. Call to Him . . . He will answer you . . . and He will show you—He will let you see—not just some things, but "great and mighty things, which you do not know."

12 DID THE DEVIL REALLY MAKE ME DO IT?

No temptation has overtaken you except such as is common to man; but God is faithful, who will not allow you to be tempted beyond what you are able, but with the temptation will also make the way of escape, that you may be able to bear it.

1 CORINTHIANS 10:13

$\mathcal{E}$arly on in my Christian pilgrimage, I discovered the value of Scripture memorization. First Corinthians 10:13 was the first verse I ever deposited in the memory bank of my mind. Because I had hidden this verse in my heart, only God has recorded how many times across the years—when I found myself faced with some sort of temptation—it surfaced in my memory and kept me from many a potential mistake. Scripture memorization plays a vital role in overcoming temptation. D. L. Moody's worn Bible, from which he preached to millions in the nineteenth century, had these words written in his own hand in the flyleaf: "The Bible will keep you from sin, or sin will keep you from the Bible."

It is not a sin to be tempted. Temptation comes our

way in all sorts of forms and sizes. Our minds are like a hotel. The manager cannot keep someone from entering the lobby. However, he can certainly keep that person from getting a room. Likewise, it is not a sin when a temptation passes through our mind. The sin comes when it does not do that, when it doesn't *pass* through our mind. The sin comes when we give that thought a room in our mind and let it dwell there.

One should not confuse temptations with trials that come our way. Most often, trials are allowed, or even sent, by God to cause the Christian to stand. Temptations are sent from the devil to cause the Christian to stumble. "Let no one say when he is tempted, 'I am tempted by God'; for God cannot be tempted by evil, nor does He Himself tempt anyone. But each one is tempted when he is drawn away by his own desires and enticed" (James 1:13–14). The devil never made us do anything. He simply dangles the bait in front of us. Then we are tempted; we are "drawn away by [our] own desires and enticed" by that which is outside the boundaries laid out for us in God's Word.

THE REALITY OF TEMPTATION
"no temptation has overtaken you except such as is common to man"

Make no mistake about it: we will be tempted. As long as we are encased in human flesh, it desires to rebel against what is good and godly. We never have to teach our children to disobey. They pick right up on it. We have to teach them to obey. So it is with us and the issue of temptation. It is a reality that is not going to go away. Consequently, it behooves us to know how to deal with temptation when it comes.

Some people live with the erroneous concept that the longer we walk the Christian path and the deeper we go with God, the less we will be tempted. None of us will ever arrive at the place when temptation will not be looming before us in some form or fashion. Most of the great heroes of the Bible faced their greatest temptations near the end of their pilgrimage rather than in the beginning. This was certainly true of Moses, Elijah, and David.

There is a word of assurance here for those who may feel a sort of pseudo guilt over being tempted: it is a reality. "No temptation has overtaken you except such as is common to man." It is inevitable. Temptation is "common to man."

THE REMINDER FOR TEMPTATION
"but God is faithful"

Life may have its shadows, but one thing is certain: they are never caused by God's turning or by His changing. He is faithful. James reminded us that "every good gift and every perfect gift is from above, and comes down from the Father of lights, with whom there is no variation or shadow of turning" (James 1:17).

Years ago, while in the process of memorizing James

1:17, I found myself one night in a parking lot standing under a light. When I stood directly under it, no shadow was cast. However, as I stepped away from the light, I began to see my shadow in front of me. The farther I walked, the larger the shadow, until finally I walked far enough to be in the darkness. The shadow was caused by my turning, my changing, and not by the light. Difficulties in life are never caused by God's turning or changing. We can rest in the reality that even though we may be tempted, we have a Lord who is faithful.

THE REMEDY FOR TEMPTATION

"[He] will not allow you to be tempted beyond what you are able, but with the temptation will also make the way of escape"

God provides a way of escape for us. The word picture here is of a mountain pass. The idea is of an army that is apparently surrounded, and then suddenly they see an escape route to safety through a mountain pass. None of us needs to succumb to the temptations that come our way. Jesus will make a way of escape. Many who have fallen into sin did so willfully because they refused to take the path of escape that the Lord put before them.

You say, "I am tempted." The Lord says, "What else is new? I, too, was tempted in all points as you, yet I was without sin" (Hebrews 4:15). Jesus taught us how to overcome our temptation. For forty days He was tempted by the devil in the wilderness of Judea. On each occurrence, Jesus overcame by quoting Scripture. The Word, hidden in our hearts, will also keep us from sin when applied by faith to our lives.

We should not be surprised when temptation comes our way. It is, after all, "common to man." But Christ Himself is our way of escape. And one thing can certainly be said of Him—"He is faithful."

As you memorize this verse this week, meditate on the words of James: "Blessed is the man who endures temptation; for when he has been approved, he will receive the crown of life which the Lord has promised to those who love Him" (James 1:12).

13 UNDERSTANDING OUR SALVATION

Being confident of this very thing, that He who has begun a good work in you will complete it until the day of Jesus Christ.

PHILIPPIANS 1:6

*M*any personal salvation testimonies go something like this: "I heard the gospel of Jesus Christ; I decided to open my life to Him; I came to Jesus; I gave Him my heart; I received Him; I repented of my sins; I decided to follow Jesus." Note the continual use of the perpendicular pronoun "I" as if it all depended upon me. When we get to heaven, we will find out how little we actually had to do with our salvation and how true our verse today is— "He who has begun a good work in you." Salvation is, from start to finish, from first to last, the work of God Himself in us. He sought us. He found us. He began the good work in us. He keeps us. And one day He will present us faultless before His Father's throne. After all, it was the shepherd himself who went after the one lost sheep until he found it, and then he carried it on his shoulders safely back to the fold, rejoicing all the while (Luke 15:1–7).

THE ORIGIN OF OUR SALVATION
"He who has begun a good work in you"

Who began the good work in you? The Lord. You reply, "I thought I did. I thought I repented. I thought I came to Christ. I thought I took the initiative." No, God did. Just as in the early chapters of Genesis, He took the skins of an innocent, sacrificial animal to cover the sin of Adam and Eve. God is still the initiator in covering our sins today. Fig leaves will not do. Solomon was on target when he said, "He who covers his sins will not prosper, but whoever confesses and forsakes them will have mercy" (Proverbs 28:13).

In our natural condition we are unresponsive to the gospel: the Bible refers to us as "dead" in our sins (Romans 6:11). We are also unperceptive; the gospel is "veiled" to us, and the god of this world has "blinded" the minds of those who do not believe (2 Corinthians 4:3–4). Without Christ, we are also unteachable: not only can we not receive the things of God, but we also consider them foolish and cannot know them because they are only spiritually discerned (1 Corinthians 2:14). Finally, we are unrighteous: we were actually shaped in iniquity and conceived in sin (Psalm 51:5). Yes, we all, like sheep, have gone away of our own accord (Isaiah 53:6).

Since being unresponsive, unperceptive, unteachable, and unrighteous is the condition in our natural state, something outside of us must intervene to enable us to become responsive to the gospel, perceptive of the things of God, teachable, and righteous before Him. Now, since we are indeed raised out of spiritual death (that is, born again) and since we are unable to perform this work on ourselves, then we must conclude it is God Himself who initiates our salvation. This is exactly what our text—"He who has begun a good work in you"—implies. God is sovereign. This simply means that He does what He pleases and He is always pleased with what He does.

The origin of our salvation lies not within us but with God Himself. He takes the initiative. He convicts us of sin. He convinces us of our righteousness in Him. He calls us out of darkness into His marvelous light. He redeems us for His own. Yes, He begins the good work in us.

THE OUTCOME OF SALVATION
"[He] will complete it until the day of Jesus Christ"

What is the outcome of this marvelous salvation provided us in Christ? It means we are secure. We are secure in the now life and in the next life as well.

We are secure in the now life. Christ, who began the good work, will finish it. He will not let us go. Since we are not *saved* by performing good works, we are not *kept* by performing good works. Paul said, "As you have therefore received Christ Jesus the Lord, so walk in Him" (Colossians 2:6). If faith is good enough to save us, it is good enough to live by, to walk in. If Christ can give us new life, He can keep us in that new life. If man takes the initiative in salvation, he must retain the responsibility for the final outcome. If God takes the initiative in salvation, then it is God who retains the responsibility for the final outcome. And, as Paul said, "He will complete it."

I remember when our first child began to learn to walk. She would reach up her chubby little fingers, grab my index finger, and hang on with all her might. She would take a step or two, let go, and fall to the ground. It didn't take me long to learn an important lesson about my role: I began to reach down and grab hold of her hand myself. Then, when she stumbled, I would be there to hold her up and keep her from falling. In the same way, our salvation is not a matter of our holding on until the bitter end. God reaches down and grabs hold of us with His strong hand. When we stumble, He is there to hold on to us and to keep us from falling. We are secure in the now life.

We are also secure in the next life. The Lord will keep and complete us "until the day of Jesus Christ." *The day of Christ* suggests that grand and glorious day when He will come again to receive us as His own. On that day the church—the body of Christ—becomes the bride of Christ. Jesus said, "This is the will of the Father who sent Me, that of all He has given Me I should lose nothing, but should raise it up at the last day" (John 6:39). Yes, we can be confident of this fact: He will keep us "until the day of Jesus

Christ." We are living now in the great "until." Until . . . the day of Jesus Christ. Until then, we can trust Him and know we are secure in the now life and in the next life that is to come.

As you memorize this verse, meditate on the fact that your salvation is, from first to last, all the doing of Him who loves you and gave Himself for you. Since He is the origin of it all, you can trust Him with the outcome of it all. As songwriter Fanny Crosby once said, "Blessed assurance, Jesus is mine!"

14 THE FORGOTTEN WORD IN OUR CHRISTIAN VOCABULARY

From that time Jesus began to preach and to say,
"Repent, for the kingdom of heaven is at hand."

MATTHEW 4:17

*T*here seems to be a forgotten word in our Christian vocabulary. The word? *Repentance.* The call to repent is strangely absent today. Some think it should be relegated to some tent service in the country, yet it was the message of all the prophets. It was the message of John the Baptist as he preached in the wilderness (Matthew 3:1–2). It was the message with which the Lord Jesus commenced His ministry (Matthew 4:17). It was also the message with which He concluded His ministry (Luke 24:46–47). It was the message of the apostles as they preached and later scattered throughout the known world (Mark 6:12). It was the message that birthed the church at Pentecost (Acts 2:37–38). It was the missionary message of the apostle Paul (Acts

17:30). And, in the last book of the Bible, it is the message of John the Revelator on Patmos to the churches of Asia (Revelation 2:5). In fact, this call to repent is woven throughout the tapestry of the entire Bible on almost every page.

Repentance is not only one of the forgotten words of our time but also one of the most misunderstood. What really is repentance? How is it applied to our lives? These are legitimate questions that deserve a definitive response in a Christian world that, in some places, is more concerned about being "seeker friendly" than biblically literate and legitimate.

JESUS' PERSONAL MANDATE COMMANDS IT *"Repent"*

This call from the lips of our Lord is not offered as an option but as a command. And that command gives rise to two important questions: *What is repentance?* and *Where is repentance?*

What is repentance? First, note what it is *not*. Repentance is not remorse. It is not simply being sorry for our sin. The rich young ruler went away "sorrowful," but he didn't repent (Luke 18:23). Repentance is not regret, or merely wishing that the deed had not happened. Pontius Pilate, who betrayed the Lord, washed his hands in regret over his turning Christ over to the crowds (Matthew 27:24). Repentance is not resolve. It is not like a New Year's resolution where we resolve to take on a new set of moral standards. And repentance is not reform—it's not just turning over a new leaf. Judas Iscariot reformed. He took the thirty pieces of silver, the payment for his betrayal of Jesus, and flung them down the corridors of the temple. Judas reformed, but he did not repent (Matthew 27:3).

Repentance comes from a Greek word that literally means "to change one's mind." It is a change of mind that affects a change of will and, in turn, brings about a change of action. This process is beautifully illustrated in the old and often repeated story of the prodigal son in Luke 15. After finding himself broke and broken, in the company of a bunch of hogs in a pig pen, the son "came to himself" (v. 17). This change of mind brought about a change of volition, a change of will. In the next verse he exclaimed, "I will arise and go to my father." Once he had changed his mind and changed his will, his actions were sure to change as well. Thus, in verse 20 we read, "And he arose and came to his father." Repentance is a change of mind. That is it. And how do we know if we have truly come to a change of mind? Our volition will be changed as well, and our changed actions will follow.

Where is repentance? That is, where is repentance in salvation? Does repentance precede faith? Or does faith come before repentance? Repentance and faith are both gifts of God's grace. They are different sides of the same coin. Charles Spurgeon, author of the classic devotional *Morning and Evening*, says they are "Siamese twins . . . vitally joined together." Repentance and faith are inseparable. Repentance alone will not get you to heaven, but you cannot get there without it. Jesus' personal mandate commands it: "Repent, for the kingdom of heaven is at hand."

JESUS' POSITIVE MOTIVE COMMENDS IT
"for the kingdom of heaven is at hand"

There is a phenomenon in America referred to as bumper-sticker evangelism. Messages are placed on the bumpers of automobiles signaling the desired message of the driver. I once saw one that read, "Turn or Burn!" However, I wonder if fear of God's punishment should be the primary motivation for calling people to repentance. Jesus used a different approach. He said, "Repent, for the kingdom of heaven is at hand." This positive motive commends the call to repentance: Jesus emphasizes the goodness of God's grace.

Paul was right on target when he said, "The goodness of God leads you to repentance" (Romans 2:4). Once, when our daughters were small, we rented a house for a week, deep in the Smokey Mountains. The first night in that strange place was "blacker than a hundred midnights down in a cypress swamp," as James Weldon Johnson, the great African American author, put it in *God's Trombones.* My wife and I were awakened in the night by the cries of our little seven-year-old at the top of the stairs. I bounded up the stairs where I found her disoriented by the darkness. Taking her by the hand, I led her downstairs into the security of our bed where she soundly slept the night away. Similarly, our dear Lord finds us in the dark, often disoriented by the issues of life, takes us by the hand, and, as the Bible says, His goodness "leads [us] to repentance."

When all is said and done, what difference does it make if we drive a luxury car, eat vitamin-enriched foods, wear expensive designer clothing, sleep on a name-brand mattress, live in a mansion on the water, and are buried in a mahogany casket in a cemetery as lovely as a botanical garden . . . only to rise up in judgment to meet a God we do not know? Jesus still calls to us, "Repent, for the kingdom of heaven is at hand." And it is His goodness that leads us to repentance. Jesus' positive motive commends His call to us to repent.

As you memorize this verse, meditate on what repentance is not . . . and then on what it is. Remember that it is the goodness of God takes you by the hand and leads you to repentance.

15 THE BIBLE: GOD'S INSPIRED WORD

All Scripture is given by inspiration of God,
and is profitable for doctrine, for reproof,
for correction, for instruction in righteousness.

2 TIMOTHY 3:16

*T*he call to memorize this verse and the intent of this chapter is not to defend the Bible. We do not have to do this. As Charles Spurgeon said, "There is no need to defend a lion when he is being attacked. All we have to do is open the gate and let him out. He will defend himself." The Bible will still be the Book of all books when all the other writings of men throughout the centuries have passed into obscurity.

Let's open the gates and let the Bible speak in its own defense. There are several important things to note.

THE DEFINED EXTENT OF AN INSPIRED BIBLE *"All Scripture..."*

The little three-letter word *all* is very inclusive. It means what it says: "*All* Scripture is given by inspiration of God." The psalmist said, "The law of the LORD is perfect" (Psalm

19:7). King Solomon said, "Every word of God is pure" (Proverbs 30:5). Some find it popular today to contend that they believe only part of the Bible, not necessarily all of it. They say, "The Bible contains the word of God, but it is not necessarily *the* word of God." But Scripture defends itself, saying, "All Scripture is given by inspiration of God."

While there are different degrees of worth in the Scripture, there are not different degrees of inspiration. One might find more personal worth in reading the Sermon on the Mount in Matthew 5–7 than in reading the genealogy tables in Matthew 1. But one passage is just as inspired as the other: "*All* Scripture" . . . is inspired. When Jesus broke forth from the obscurity of the Nazareth carpentry shop to begin His public ministry, He was immediately tempted by the devil, and He replied with the Scripture: "It is written, 'Man shall not live by bread alone, but by every word that proceeds from the mouth of God'" (Matthew 4:4). To what extent is the Bible inspired? The answer to that question is found in the first two words of our verse for the week: "All Scripture . . ."

THE DETAILED EVIDENCE OF AN INSPIRED BIBLE

"given by inspiration of God"

The Scripture is "given." It is supernatural. It is given by God. It originates with God, not with man. It is a library of sixty-six books written over a period of more than fourteen hundred years by at least forty different authors from all walks of life. Some were fishermen, and others were prophets, kings, shepherds, doctors, and rabbis. Yet this Book has come together with one theology, one plan of redemption, and one theme running throughout its pages, leaving no explanation for its unique nature outside of God Himself. It is "given" by God Himself.

And it is "given by inspiration." This phrase literally means "God breathed." God used men in the process, but He did not breathe on them. Instead, He breathed out of them His Word. Just as a skilled musical composer creates a score utilizing the flute, the trumpet, and other instruments, so God chose His own instruments. Some were as different as flutes are from trumpets. Yet God chose those instruments and breathed out His Word to us through them.

Inspiration means the words are God's words, and He gave them to man through man. Peter said that "holy men of God spoke as they were moved by the Holy Spirit" (2 Peter 1:21). Ironically, the identical Greek word translated here as "moved" appears in the account of Paul's shipwreck recorded in Acts 27. There came a fierce storm, and the sailors onboard, unable to guide the ship because of the strong winds, simply let the winds take the ship wherever they blew it (vv. 15 and 17). Just as the sailors were active on the ship, yet had relinquished control over where it would go, so it was with the Bible writers. In a very real sense, the writings were not their own. God Himself expressed this very point to Jeremiah: "I have put My words in your mouth" (Jeremiah 1:9). The Bible does not originate with men; it originates with God. The writers' personalities and styles are unique to them, but it was God who moved them to write by His Spirit. "All Scripture is given by inspiration of God."

THE DIVINE EFFECT OF AN INSPIRED BIBLE *"is profitable for doctrine, for reproof, for correction, for instruction in righteousness"*

God's Word is indeed "profitable" for these four things. There is a sense in which the Bible is like a roadmap. First there is doctrine, the way we begin our journey with proper teaching that shows us God's plan of salvation and sanctification. But what happens if something causes us to veer off the road? The Bible is then profitable for reproof: it shows us our wrong turn. God asks, "Is not My word . . . like a hammer that breaks the rock in pieces?" (Jeremiah 23:29). However, the Bible does not leave us in our reproof. Next, the Bible is profitable for correction: it corrects our mistakes and gets us on the road again. Finally, Scripture is profitable for "instruction in righteousness": the Word instructs us how to stay on the road so that we do not get off again.

We see the divine effects of an inspired Bible throughout the writings of Paul in the New Testament. He wrote the letter to the Romans to emphasize the importance of doctrine. His letters to the Corinthians are profitable for reproof. In the Galatian epistle, his emphasis was on correction. And, in the Ephesian letter, Paul spoke of the need for "instruction in righteousness."

An effective ministry of God's Word will do all four—teach doctrine, reprove sin, correct false paths, and instruct in godly living. Balance is the key. Some believers go overboard on doctrine to the virtual exclusion of reproof, correction, or instruction. Even though these folks are doctrinally sound, they are living without power. Others focus too much on reproof: they seem to think it is their God-given assignment to reprove everyone else about their sin. Others focus on correction, apparently thinking it is their calling to correct everyone else. Still others get out of balance on "instruction in righteousness" to the exclusion of teaching doctrine, and thus they have no direction in life. An effective Christian life is a balanced life.

The desired end of knowing Scripture is that "the man of God may be complete, thoroughly equipped for every good work" (2 Timothy 3:17).

As you memorize this verse, meditate on the fact that, when you study the Bible, you do not judge it; it judges you. God's Word has withstood the test of time and will still be the Book of all books when all others have passed into obscurity. No wonder the psalmist said, "Your word I have hidden in my heart, that I might not sin against You" (Psalm 119:11).

16 VISION IS VITAL

Where there is no revelation, the people cast off restraint;
But happy is he who keeps the law.

PROVERBS 29:18

⬧⬧⬧⬧⬧⬧⬧⬧⬧⬧⬧⬧⬧⬧

*V*ision is vital to Christian living. Those who grew up memorizing the King James Version of the Bible remember this verse translated as, "Where there is no vision, the people perish." According to Strong's Hebrew Lexicon, the word *revelation* (vision) means "to mentally perceive; to contemplate." The word translated *restraint* or *perish* is translated other places in the Old Testament as "to go back." We see this in Numbers 14:3 (NIV) when those wandering in the wilderness wanted to "go back" to Egypt. Thus, those who have no vision, no perception of what they could be, seem to have no real direction in their Christian pilgrimage.

Vision is vital. Soon after the completion of Disney World in Orlando, someone asked Michael Vance, the creative director, "Isn't it too bad Walt Disney did not live to see this?" Vance quickly replied, "He did see it, and that is precisely why we are here today!" If this is true for secular organizations, how much more vital is vision for those of us who are seeking to be followers of Christ, the greatest visionary who ever lived?

Before every great undertaking, there is someone who has a vision for the task ahead. The football coach has a game plan before the kickoff, a vision of what he wants his team to accomplish. The army commander or platoon leader sees the infantry's strategy, a battle plan, before the fighting ever begins. The artist has a conception in his or her mind before the painting is put on the canvas. What a difference vision makes in life. Too many Christians are just going to meetings, following schedules, simply existing—and something is missing. Vision, a perception of what God wants us to be and do, is vital. When a believer discovers God's vision for life, that vision will do five things.

VISION BRINGS DEFINITION

When we truly capture the vision of what God wants us to be and do, that vision serves to define our task. Many go so far as to formulate a one-sentence vision statement for their lives. This becomes the lens through which they view their choices and make their decisions. Churches need vision statements. For example, one church has a vision statement that says they are making "a great commitment to the Great Commandment and the Great Commission." Thus, church leaders keep their ministries in perspective by filtering them through the lens that serves as a reminder that if something does not lend itself to loving God, loving others, and leading men and women to saving faith in Jesus Christ, it does not make their priority list. Vision brings definition; it defines our decisions.

VISION BRINGS DESIGN

This design is seen in the way vision is accomplished. The birth of a vision is like the birth of a baby. The first step is conception. This takes place when a seed of what God wants us to be is planted in our hearts by the Lord Himself. The next state is gestation. Here we "gestate" the vision, think about it, and pray over it for a period of time. After a while those close to us see that something is happening, that we are pregnant with a vision. Next comes the birth: the vision is born and is out there for all to see. Then comes the most important step for leaders, the stage of adoption. Here the vision, which has not been personally conceived or gestated, much less born to them, is adopted by others and, by all rights, belongs to them. Leaders know the next stage is growth. Growing kids cost money and time, and so do growing visions. Next follows maturity when all that we have dreamed of and prayed for reaches maturity. Finally there comes the stage of reproduction, when previous visions are reproduced into newer and more expanded visions, and the dream goes on. Vision brings design to life.

VISION BRINGS DYNAMIC

Not much really happens without a vision. Dynamics and motivation are lacking. Nothing was happening in Jerusalem until Nehemiah's vision took on definition and design. Then it brought a new dynamic as he returned to become the rebuilder of the broken walls. Vision is what brings a dynamic and a sense of conquest to our work and witness as believers.

VISION BRINGS DIRECTION

One of the most important things a personal vision can bring is direction to our lives. "Where are you headed?" is a valid question. When a personal vision is guiding our lives, bringing a new sense of dynamic, it will also bring a new sense of purpose and direction.

VISON BRINGS DEPENDENCE

One of the spiritually beneficial things that vision brings to a life is a new sense of dependence upon the Lord. Visions should be so God-sized that there is no way for them to be accomplished unless God intervenes.

The Lord doesn't see us for what we are now. When He first met Simon Peter, He saw the fisherman as a small pebble. However, Jesus then said that Peter would become a great rock. It was an effective play on words. Christ saw the potential that was within Peter. God sees us not so much for what we are now but for what we could be—if, that is, we receive a vision from Him for the work at hand. Vision brings definition, design, dynamic, direction, and dependence: "Where there is no revelation (no vision of what God wants us to be and do), the people cast off restraint (they go back)."

As you memorize this verse this week, meditate on the fact that the birth of a vision does not just happen. It must be conceived in the secret place alone with God, then gestated—prayed over and contemplated upon—until it is birthed. "Where there is no vision, the people perish" (Proverbs 29:18 KJV). Develop your own vision of what it is God wants you to be and do. It will begin when it is conceived in the secret place with Him. Then, after a period of spiritual gestation, it will be birthed!

17 IS JESUS STILL WEEPING?

Jesus wept.

JOHN 11:35

W̲e now come to the shortest verse in all the Bible. Without question, it is the easiest to memorize. It contains only two words, three syllables. However, these two words offer incredible insight into the heart of our Lord. For those of us who attended Vacation Bible School as children, more than likely this was among the first verses we put to memory—"Jesus wept."

There are two passages in Scripture that reveal our Lord actually weeping. Ironically, both of them take place on the Mount of Olives opposite Jerusalem. On the eastern slope of the mountain, in the small village of Bethany, we find Jesus weeping over our sorrows at the grave of Lazarus (John 11:35). On the western slope of the mountain, we find Him on Palm Sunday weeping over our sins (Luke 19:41). One can't help but wonder when we read these words if Jesus is still weeping today. Tears have a language all their own. The tears of our Lord speak volumes to us in this dispensation of grace.

JESUS WEEPS OVER OUR SORROWS: HE IS TOUCHED BY OUR BROKEN HEARTS

The event was the funeral of His close friend Lazarus. With poignant brevity, John simply states, "Jesus wept." He did not weep because Lazarus was dead. He knew that in a moment He could restore life to him—and those who know the Bible know this is exactly what He did! Jesus wept when He saw Lazarus's sisters crying. Tears touch the heart of our God. Mary's heart was broken. Her brother was dead, and it seemed Jesus had arrived too late. She held no hope. She was hurting. She was weeping with deep sobs and wails. She was pouring out her soul to the Lord. When Jesus saw her, He wept with her. This great God is touched by our own hurts and broken hearts.

Tears have a language all their own. They speak much louder than words. They need no interpreter. The psalmist says that God keeps our tears in a bottle (Psalm 56:8). If you need God's attention, try tears. It is okay to cry. We serve a Lord who weeps with us over our sorrows and who is touched by our broken hearts.

JESUS WEEPS OVER OUR SINS: HE IS TROUBLED BY OUR BLINDED EYES

Most messages related to the Palm Sunday event have to do with the crowds, the shouts of the hosannas, the parade, the pep rally. But all that was a sham. And our Lord knew it. Within a few short days, those same crowds would disappear, and their cheers would be turned to jeers. Can you picture Him that day, on the back of a donkey, riding over palm branches to the praise of the people? He was the center of attention. He must have been smiling from ear to ear and waving at the adoring crowds like He was sitting in a convertible on a parade route. But look closer: "Now as He drew near, He saw the city and wept over it" (Luke 19:41). Hear Him through His tears as He says, "If you had known, even you, especially in this your day, the things that make for your peace! But now they are hidden from your eyes" (v. 42).

Those Jerusalem crowds wanted a military general who would ride into town and put down the Roman oppressors. Thus, less than a week after the grand parade, when they realized they were not getting what they wanted, they crowned Him King all right, but with a crown of thorns. They stripped Him naked, beat Him, and asked, "Are you the King of the Jews?" *What a joke*, they thought. And they laughed. He was, in fact, a King, but His kingdom was not of this world. His is the kingdom of our hearts. And so our Lord Jesus sat on the Mount of Olives and wept. Interestingly, a different Greek word is used to describe His weeping on the Palm Sunday road than His weeping at Bethany. The word here entails a loud sobbing, groaning, and cries that could be heard a block away. Jesus poured out His heart over our spiritual neglect and sin.

Sadly, those of us in the Western church today do not seem to be weeping over the sins of those around us or even our own sins. We are hardly troubled by blinded eyes. We are watching the decay of a civilization before us. This is America in the twenty-first century, and Jesus is still weeping . . . but many of us are not. Many of us have lost our tears, but tears speak so much louder than words.

The Lord Jesus is still touched by our broken hearts and troubled by our blinded eyes. Is our Lord weeping *with* you or *over* you today? There is, after all, a huge difference between the two.

The last time tears are mentioned in the Bible is in Revelation 21:4. It reveals a beautiful scene in heaven: "God will wipe away every tear from their eyes." This is our hope. He is preserving all our tears in a bottle, and one day He will wipe them all away. King David said it best: "For His anger is but for a moment, His favor is for life; weeping may endure for a night, but joy comes in the morning" (Psalm 30:5).

As you memorize this verse this week, meditate on the fact that we have a Lord who is not far off and removed. He is very near. He is the One who is touched by our broken hearts and weeps with us. And He is the One who is troubled by our blinded eyes and weeps over us. These two little words speak volumes: "Jesus wept." It is okay to cry.

18 LIFE'S BOTTOM-LINE QUESTION

*"I am the resurrection and the life. He who believes
in Me, though he may die, he shall live."*

JOHN 11:25

*T*his one statement is among the most bold and definitive acknowledgments of our Lord's deity. The resurrection is what separates our Lord from a thousand other gurus and prophets who have come down the pike. This bold declaration is then followed, in the next verse, by life's bottom-line question. After declaring Himself to be the resurrection and life, the victor over death, our Lord turns to His hearers—and to us—and asks, "Do you believe this?" (John 11:26).

One of the frustrations of Scripture reading is that, like other writings, it is all linear. Thus, I have often wondered how Jesus spoke this question. Did He ask, "Do *you* believe this?" Or did He ask, "Do you *believe* this?" Or perhaps He asked the question thus: "Do you believe *this*?" Think about it. Life's bottom-line question is personal, pointed, and precise.

LIFE'S BOTTOM-LINE QUESTION IS PERSONAL *"Do YOU believe this?"*

Perhaps the Lord put the inflection on the *you* in His question in order to drive home the fact that it is personal. After all, when it comes to saving faith in the finished work of Christ, what I believe is what matters most . . . not what my mother or my wife or anyone else believes. My faith is a personal matter between my Lord and me.

In our twenty-first-century gnostic culture, an increasing number of individuals seems to be captivated by various documentaries, movies, and books that question the veracity of the gospel account. To many, the account of the resurrection has been relegated to some ancient shelf of obscurity along with other perceived myths and fables. Thus, life's bottom-line question is personal. It might well be that Jesus is still asking today: Do *you* believe this?

LIFE'S BOTTOM-LINE QUESTION IS POINTED *"Do you BELIEVE this?"*

It may be that in asking this question, our Lord put added inflection and emphasis on the word *believe*. After all, faith is the acceptable response to the Christian gospel. Jesus was not inquiring of His hearers as to whether they were giving intellectual assent to His claims. He wanted to know if they would trust in Him and take Him at His word by faith: Do you *believe* this?

It is one thing to know the gospel story intellectually. It is one thing to attempt to conform ourselves to its claims and seek to take on the new set of moral standards that accompanies its truths. It is even one thing to argue for it apologetically and reason about it. It is, in fact, possible to conform to its claims without being transformed from within by grace and through faith.

Life's bottom-line question is pointed. Jesus begs to know if you have transferred your own trust from human efforts to Him alone. Has this saving faith, this resurrected life, this "Christ in me" experience made a difference in your life? Jesus said, "I am the resurrection and the life." Do you *believe* this?

LIFE'S BOTTOM-LINE QUESTION IS PRECISE *"Do you believe* THIS?"

Now we arrive at the real heart of the issue. True faith must rest on objective truth. Thus, life's bottom-line question is precise at four very specific points related to Jesus' claim "I am the resurrection and the life, He who believes in Me, though he may die, he shall live. And whoever lives and believes in Me shall never die." Do you believe *this*?

Do you believe Jesus' claim about *deity*? When Christ used the phrase *I am*, it captured the attention of those around Him. Seven times the "I am" expression is recorded in John's gospel. Whenever our Lord made this statement, those around Him recognized it as an expression of His deity. He was the same God, named "I AM," who appeared in Exodus 3 at the burning bush. The most fundamental belief in the Christian faith is that Jesus Christ is God Himself clothed in human flesh. He is not merely some figure out of history or the object of some sentimental story from our childhood. He is God. Do you believe *this*?

Do you believe His claim about *death*? Jesus said, "Though he may die, he shall live." Many people live their lives in total denial of their coming appointment with death. It is a fact: we are going to die! Recently, while looking through some pictures from a decade or so ago, I was stunned. My hair was darker then. My face had fewer wrinkles. It dawned on me that this body of mine has death in it. I am decaying and deteriorating before my very eyes. Oh, I could have plastic surgery or perhaps some liposuction. I can eat vitamin-enriched foods and try to keep my cholesterol down. But none of that can stop the fact that I continue marching toward an appointment with eternity. Do you believe *this*?

Do you believe His claim about *destiny*? Jesus said, "Though he may die, he shall live." It is strange how so many today live their lives as if this life is all there is. Jesus said that even though death is sure, we are going to live again. The body may die, but not the spirit, not that part of you that will live as long as God lives and will one day be reunited with a glorified body for the endless ages of eternity. We have an eternal destiny. Do you believe *this*?

Do you believe His claim about *deliverance*? Jesus says, "Whoever lives and believes in Me shall never die" (John 11:26). The Lord makes it perfectly plain here. Eternal salvation is through faith in Him alone and not through human effort or our own good works or intentions. Do you believe *this*?

There are a lot of big questions that come our way in life. Where will I attend college? Whom shall I marry? What vocation shall I pursue? Where should I live? But there is only one big question in death: "Do you believe this?" That's it! It is personal. Do *you* believe this? It is pointed. Do you *believe* this? And, it is precise. Do you believe *this*?

Finally, note Martha's reply in the next verse: "Yes, Lord, I believe that You are the Christ, the Son of God, who is to come into the world" (John 11:27).

As you memorize this verse, meditate on Martha's reply. Would you join her by simply professing to Him, "Yes, Lord, I believe that You are the Christ!" And then you will begin the great adventure for which you were created in the first place.

19 GOD'S RECIPE FOR REVIVAL

"If My people who are called by My name will humble themselves, and pray and seek My face, and turn from their wicked ways, then I will hear from heaven, and will forgive their sin and heal their land."

2 CHRONICLES 7:14

*D*uring a recent Christmas season, while I was passing through our kitchen where my wife was busy preparing the big family meal, my eyes fell on an old notecard that had yellowed with the years. Looking closely, I saw my mother's handwriting on it. It was her old recipe for one of my favorite dishes. When done precisely as the directions said, it tasted exactly like my mother used to make it!

Within the heart of each of us is a longing for something more, a season of new spiritual refreshing, a personal revival, if you please. God has His own recipe for revival in our hearts. He has written it down for all of us: "If My people will . . . then I will hear from heaven." And when this recipe is followed precisely and put into practice, it will result in a new spirit reanimating us and enabling us to soar into spiritual regions some of us may have never known.

Much talk of revival is from man's side, man's viewpoint. Thus, it becomes man-centered. For a moment, let's seek to transport ourselves and view personal revival from the throne of God. That is, from God's viewpoint.

GOD'S DESIRE *"If My people . . . then . . ."*

God is waiting, willing, and longing to send a new spirit of revival to His people. However, He does not overrule our own will. Consequently, in a very real sense, while revival is always the sovereign work of Almighty God, it is also conditional. The Bible says, "*If* My people . . ." If certain conditions are met, certain results will follow.

God longs to send revival to us: "He is not willing that any perish" (2 Peter 3:9). There is a very real sense in which personal revival is not a miracle. It is simply God's promised response to conditions met by His people.

GOD'S DESIGN *"If MY people . . ."*

Revival is conditional upon God's own people. Hear His invitation: "If *My* people . . ." The real story behind any revival in history begins when God's own people become convicted of neglect and begin to beseech the throne for a fresh wind of His Spirit. Reading the history of many great awakenings reveals that they usually begin with one man or one woman who becomes desperate for what the psalmist called "fresh oil" (Psalm 92:10).

God's problem today is not with the lost but with His

own people. Many are pointing to the decay of our culture as being the result of the decline of our moral fabric and the influence of secular, and often downright godless factors all around us. However, God reveals that the real issue is not with "them" but with "us." Or, as Jesus once said, we should not try to get a small splinter out of someone else's eye until we first remove the large beam from our own eye (Matthew 7:3–5). God's design for revival begins with His own people.

GOD'S DEMAND *"humble themselves, and pray and seek My face, and turn from their wicked ways"*

God's demand begins with a call for His own people to "humble themselves," to recognize and confess their need to seek Him in all things. The Christian must be on constant vigil to avoid the temptation of spiritual pride and self-centeredness. True humility involves a broken spirit before the Lord.

Second, God calls His people to pray. The word does not entail the mere recitation of prayers but an earnest calling out to Him. Too many Christians' prayer testimonies can be summed up with four words from Ephesians 6:12—"we do not wrestle." Every true revival in history has been born and cradled in the place of prayer. We read of the early church that "when they had prayed, the place where they were assembled together was shaken; and they were all filled with the Holy Spirit, and they spoke the word of God with boldness" (Acts 4:31).

Next, God demands that we "seek [His] face." He said to Jeremiah, "You will seek Me and find Me, when you search for Me with all your heart" (Jeremiah 29:13). If believers today spent as much time seeking His face as we do seeking His hand, we would be on the way to revival. Much of our own praying seems to be consumed with seeking something from His hand in the way of material or physical needs. Perhaps too little of our praying is consumed with simply seeking His face for personal revival.

God's demand also includes turning from our "wicked ways." Sin that is unconfessed and therefore unforgiven is the greatest obstacle to revival. As Solomon reminded us, "He who covers his sins will not prosper, but whoever confesses and forsakes them will have mercy" (Proverbs 28:13). Note that it is not enough to simply be sorry for and to confess our sins; we must also forsake them.

GOD'S DELIGHT *"I will hear from heaven, and will forgive their sin and heal their land."*

God's delight is to forgive and cleanse us of our sin. Why? So that we might appropriate all that the cross of Christ involves, so that, as far as we might personally be concerned, His death would not be in vain. God delights more in healing our hearts and our homes than we do ourselves.

He is willing, waiting, and longing to be faithful because of conditions we are called to meet.

If my daughter and I had a misunderstanding or something had broken our fellowship, I would long for restoration. If she came to me in humility, asked for forgiveness, and looked lovingly into my face, how do you think I would react? Of course I would forgive her and welcome her with open arms and an open heart. No wonder the Bible reveals that our heavenly Father will do so much more for us! This great God, who sees a small field sparrow when it falls to earth, cares much more for you (Matthew 6:25–27, 10:29).

As you memorize this verse, meditate on the fact that personal revival, while it is God's work, is also conditional: "If My people . . . then I will hear from heaven." God has a recipe for personal revival. Our part is not that difficult. It simply calls us to follow the directions.

20   OH, THAT SAGGING MIDDLE!

I have been crucified with Christ; it is no longer I
who live, but Christ lives in me; and the life which
I now live in the flesh I live by faith in the Son of God,
who loved me and gave Himself for me.

GALATIANS 2:20

$\mathcal{M}$y father's family came to Texas from Tennessee back in the 1800s. When I was a boy in the 1950s, each summer we would make our annual trek back to Tennessee to visit my Great Aunt Ann. I loved those long car trips in the days before the interstate highways. We would stay in her house, and I would sleep in an old iron bed on a feather mattress. Anyone who has had a similar experience knows that several times during the night you awaken in a ball in the middle of that soft feather mattress. I once heard Stuart Briscoe refer to the Christian life as a soft mattress. I can relate. That bed was extremely firm on both iron ends; but, oh, that sagging middle.

A lot of Christians live their lives like that old iron bedstead with the soft feathered mattress. That is, they are firm on both ends. They are firm on the front end: they know that, at a certain point in time, they put their trust in Christ and have the assurance that they have been born again. They are also firm on the other end: they know they are going to heaven when they die. But, oh, that sagging middle; those years in between for beating out the principles of the Christian life on the anvil of personal, daily experiences. And that middle often seems to be sagging.

Galatians 2:20 is the secret to firming up the middle of our walk with Christ. This was the second verse I remember memorizing as a teenage believer. I knew after my conversion that something grand and glorious had taken place within me. I asked one of my new Christian friends, "What happened to me?" He pointed me to Galatians 2:20. I memorized it that day and have held it close to my heart as one of my life verses throughout the years of my own Christian experience. This is one of the most personal verses in the entire Bible. Like a spring meadow with its buzzing visitors, the verse swarms with personal pronouns. (There are seven personal pronouns in all, depending upon the English version.) This single verse is perhaps the most complete description of the Christian life to be found in the New Testament. It reveals to us what Christ has done for us.

HE TOOK SOMETHING FROM ME: MY OLD LIFE
"I have been crucified with Christ;"

In this statement of Paul's, the verb tense is perfect;

that is, the action has been completed in the past with continuing results. The mood is passive; that is, the subject is the recipient of the action—all because of Christ. After all, we cannot crucify ourselves. We might get a hand nailed or a foot nailed to our cross, but we cannot crucify ourselves. The statement is also in the indicative, meaning that it is a simple statement of known fact. The apostle went beyond simply saying that Christ was crucified *for* me. He said I was crucified *with* Christ. It is a statement of fact. Jesus did it, not me. It was done long ago, but it has a continuing effect today.

When Dr. R. G. Lee, the late, great preacher of the gospel, first went on a pilgrimage to Jerusalem, he and his tour group came to Golgotha, the place of the crucifixion. Lee, moved with emotion, ran ahead of the crowd. When they caught up with him at that sacred spot, they found him kneeling with tears streaming down his cheeks. "Oh, Dr. Lee, I see you have been here before," remarked one of the group. "No . . . Yes . . . Yes, I have been here before. Almost two thousand years ago." And then the old preacher quoted Galatians 2:20.

As the Lord Jesus hung on Calvary's cross, those in the crowd saw only one man on that center cross. But God the Father saw not just Christ but you and all others who would put their faith in Him hanging there. When we come to Christ, God takes our old life from us. We are "crucified with Christ." In the first-century world, a person carrying a cross meant only one thing: he was going to die. We are to take up our cross and live like dead men and women today, dead to our old lives and alive to a new life in Christ.

HE PUT SOMETHING IN ME: MY NEW LIFE

"it is no longer I who live, but Christ lives in me;"

The new life in Christ is not a reformed life. It is not an improved life. It is not even a changed life. It is an *ex*changed life. We give God our old life, and He gives us one that is brand new. The apostle Paul had died to his old self-centered life and awakened to a new life in Christ. While many say, "Not Christ, but I," the believer says, "Not I, but Christ!"

Think of this awesome thought: "Christ lives in me." If we could literally awaken to this revelation, we would be on the way to turning our "world upside down" like those who went before us in the early church (Acts 17:6). There is no way to defeat a man who truly believes that Christ is alive and has taken up permanent residency in him.

HE GAVE SOMETHING FOR ME: HIS OWN LIFE

"[He] loved me and gave Himself for me."

There are two realities I wish the whole world could know: God loves you and He gave Himself for you. These verbs are punctiliar; that is, at a point in time God's great love took Him to the cross, and there He willingly gave Himself for you.

Think of it: "He loved me." If I asked Paul how it is that He loved me, he would fire back without batting an eye, "He . . . gave Himself for you." Jesus proved His love. He died in my place. His love took my sin so that I could take His righteousness. His love died my death so that I could live His life. He gave Himself for *me*! What a Savior!

Perhaps your life is like my Great Aunt Ann's old iron bed: firm on both ends, but sagging in the middle. You can firm up the middle by coming to the reality of this one verse and incarnating it.

As you memorize this verse, meditate on the words written by Elizabeth Clephane over one hundred fifty years ago in her old song of the faith:

> "I take, O cross, thy shadow for my abiding place;
> I ask no other sunshine than the sunshine of
>   His face;
> Content to let the world go by, to know no gain
>   nor loss;
> My sinful self, my only shame; my glory—
>   all the cross."

21 GONE FISHING

"Follow Me, and I will make you become fishers of men."

MARK 1:17 NASB

*F*ollow Me. Those were two words spoken so often by our Lord. He came upon a group of fishermen who were engrossed in their lifetime fishing business, looked them squarely in the eyes, and called them to put away their nets and follow Him on a life-transforming journey. In Capernaum, Jesus saw a Jew taking up tax money for the Roman oppressors. Again, He spoke those two simple words, and Matthew put down his money pouch and followed after Him. Over and over in the Gospels we hear this simple call. When we heed Jesus' call today and become His followers, we then become interested in what He is interested in. Jesus revealed to us that He had "come to seek and to save that which was lost" (Luke 19:10). The truth is, if we are genuinely following Jesus, we are also fishing.

It has always been of peculiar interest to me that, when it came time to pick His team, whom He would train and then send out with a commission to reach entire nations, Jesus picked rough, callous-handed men who had spent their lives in the fishing business. He did not go to the institutions of higher learning looking for the best and the brightest. He did not go to the halls of government looking for those with gifted persuasive powers. He did not go to the yeshivas and pick those most knowledgeable in the Torah. He went to Galilee, to a bunch of ragtag fishermen, and called them to follow Him with the promise that He would make them become "fishers of men." Why them? Why fishermen?

My family and I lived on the Atlantic coast for fifteen years among many people whose livelihoods were related to fishing. On occasion I would take a seaplane from Fort Lauderdale to the little island of Bimini in search of the elusive bonefish of the Bimini flats, pound for pound the greatest sport fish anywhere. My guide was always the legendary "Bonefish Sam" Ellis. He was old even then, but he could still spot a dorsal fin from a football field away. We would fish all day under the blistering island sun. Once, while on my way home, flying back toward the sunset, I wrote down a few words in my journal to describe this seasoned legend of the flats. It dawned on me that what I saw in Bonefish Sam is what Jesus is looking for in His followers today. *And these traits are at the very heart of why He called fishermen to follow Him.*

A REAL FISHERMAN IS POSITIVE

As we left the dock, Sam would always exclaim something to the effect of, "Today is the day! There is a world-record bonefish out there just waiting for us to catch him!" He was so positive that by the time we got to the fishing location, I was so pumped up I was already thinking about where I would place my mounted world-record catch. This attitude is characteristic of all real fishermen. A real fisherman is always just one cast away from landing the big one.

And this is the type of person Jesus calls to follow Him. He is after those who are positive, those who see an answer in every problem, not those who look for problems in every answer. A real fisherman is positive.

A REAL FISHERMAN IS PERSISTENT

Bonefish Sam was persistency personified! By noon one day, we had been blistered by the sun, battered by the waves, and, to top it off, had not seen the first bonefish. I was ready to go back to the dock, sit under the cool of a palm tree, and enjoy a good lunch. Not Sam Ellis! Winston Churchill must have learned his famous "never give up" philosophy from Bonefish Sam. We kept at it through the noon hour and into the late afternoon until we landed a big one.

This is exactly the type of person the Lord Jesus knew it would take to transform the world. He goes after those who are not simply positive but persistent. He calls folks who have a "never give up" attitude, who keep on keeping on, regardless of the circumstances or situation. A real fisherman is persistent.

A REAL FISHERMAN IS PATIENT

On the flight back that night, the word *patient* quickly came to mind. I jotted it down. Sam was never in a hurry. He revealed to me that day that my own impatience would keep me from ever becoming a true fisherman. I also noted that, being patient, he was willing to try different methods. If one bait was not working, he put on another. He was not locked into just one way of doing his thing. Flexibility was his password, and in the end it paid off handsomely.

Jesus knew when He called those fishermen to follow Him that one of their common characteristics was patience. They could not have spent their lives at this trade without it. He knew that those who followed Him would have to be patient in future times when the situation would appear hopeless. Jesus is still looking for men and women who are not locked into one way of doing things. He desires us to be willing to try different methods as we fish for the souls of men. Jesus knows that a real fisherman is patient.

A REAL FISHERMAN IS PASSIONATE

As the little seaplane's tires screeched and bounced down the home runway, I hurriedly wrote down one more word—*passionate*. Earlier that afternoon, we had fought a large bonefish for almost half an hour. Finally, when it was within ten feet of the boat and a few hours from the taxidermist, it jumped out of the water, spit the hook in our direction, and swam away. Sam had a fisherman's fit. I learned that day that a real fisherman is passionate. He hates to lose one!

This is the type of person Jesus wants on His team. He is still calling passionate people to follow Him. He longs for His followers to, like Bonefish Sam, always hate to lose one.

I often think of Bonefish Sam Ellis when recruiting men and women to become a part of my team. I want people around me like that crusty old fisherman of the Bimini flats. Learning from our Lord, I try to look for those who are positive, persistent, patient, and passionate.

As you memorize this verse, meditate on the wonder that the Lord Jesus still uses ordinary people like you and me to do extraordinary things for His glory. Be positive; start looking for an answer in every problem. Be persistent; never give up. Be patient; try some different methods. And be passionate; always hate to lose one! Jesus said, "Follow Me, and I will make you become fishers of men."

22 TRUE CONFESSION

If we confess our sins, He is faithful and just to forgive us our sins and to cleanse us from all unrighteousness.

1 JOHN 1:9

❦❦❦❦❦❦❦❦❦❦❦

*I*n the first epistle that bears his name, John was writing to believers. Thirty times in these five short chapters, he used the word *know* in order to drive home the reality that we can have assurance of the salvation freely offered to us by the Lord Jesus Christ. This is the same John who once was a carefree Galilean fisherman, who eventually made his way into our Lord's inner circle along with his brother James and Simon Peter. This is the same John who leaned upon the Lord's breast during the Last Supper in the Upper Room. And it is the same faithful follower who stood with Mary at the foot of the cross when all the others had forsaken Jesus and fled (Mark 14:50).

Now John drives home to our hearts one of the real secrets of maintaining fellowship with Christ, and that is the forgiveness of sins. The word translated *forgive* in our English versions finds its origin in a Greek word that means "to send away." The same word is used when describing the scapegoat that was sent away by the high priest into the wilderness, symbolically taking with it the sins of the people of Israel. It is also the word used in detailing how the fever left a certain person after the touch of Jesus. And it is God's desire to send away our sins from us. He has provided a way, and this is the issue at hand in 1 John 1:9. Here we discover how to get our sins sent away so that, as the psalmist said, they may be separated from us "as far as the east is from the west" and remembered no more (Psalm 103:12).

FORGIVENESS IS CONDITIONAL
"If we confess our sins"

Many of God's promises are conditional on certain requirements to be met by His children. In this devotional we have already seen this truth in 2 Chronicles 7:14: "If My people . . . will humble themselves . . . then I will hear from heaven." The forgiveness talked about in 1 John 1:9 all hinges upon the "Big If": "if we confess our sins." Thus, we are immediately confronted with the reality that the forgiveness of our sins is conditional upon the confession of our sins.

The word *confession* is a compound word in the language of the New Testament. It comes from a word meaning "to say" and another meaning "the same as." Confession literally means that "we say the same as God" about our sin. We agree with Him regarding it. Sin is not some little vice that we can laugh off. It is not something we can excuse by saying everyone is doing it. It is not some sort of mistake that we can minimize by trying to convince ourselves that it is not as bad as the sins many others commit. Sin is so serious that it necessitated the cross. Often, our own guilt is God's way of saying, "You have sinned." Confession, then, is our way of saying, "I agree with You, God. I have sinned."

FORGIVENESS IS CONFESSIONAL
"confess"

As we have seen above, confession is agreeing with God about our sin. We say, "Oh, that is not worry; it is simply concern." We say, "That is not anger; it is righteous indignation." We say, "That is not lust. Just an appreciative glance." But confession does not say those things. Confession agrees with God about our sin. What we may camouflage as concern, God calls the sin of worry. What we may refer to as righteous indignation, God, who knows our hearts, calls it the sin of anger. What we may try to say is just an admiring glance, God calls the sin of lust in our heart. Confession gets open and honest with God, and there is no forgiveness without it.

Anyone who has raised children has had the occasion of a spilled glass of milk at the breakfast table. Think about it. The glass tumbles over. The mother exclaims, "What happened?" Everyone scrambles to stand up and starts mopping the table with the napkins . . .

except the guilty one who sheepishly asks, "Yeah, what happened?" And so here we are. We cheat on a business deal, and God asks, "What happened?" We reply, "Oh, it was the pressure of the economy." Someone gets into an illicit affair, and God asks, "What happened?" We reply, "It was simply one of those inevitable things that just happened." But confession says, "I knocked over the glass . . . I cheated someone else . . . I perpetrated the sin of passion . . . I am to blame . . . I take responsibility." Confession agrees with God on the matter. It does not say, "*If* I have sinned." It confesses, "I have sinned." The good news is that Jesus Christ died on the cross bearing our sins in His own body and taking the punishment for them all. Forgiveness is free to all . . . but it is conditional and confessional.

FORGIVENESS IS CONTINUAL
"If we confess our sins"

Note carefully it is our *sins* that are at issue here and not our *sin nature*. God deals with our sin in 1 John 1:7 saying, "But if we walk in the light as He is in the light, we have fellowship with one another, and the blood of Jesus Christ His Son cleanses us from all sin." Sin is singular here because the verse refers to our sin nature that Christ dealt with on the cross. There are important distinctions between the root (sin) and the fruit (sins). First John 1:9 deals with our sins—which we are to continually confess when we are made aware of them through conviction in our hearts.

Our *sin* was dealt with on Calvary. When we were converted to Christ, we did not have to confess all our *sins*. Who of us could remember through all the years a fraction of them? It is our sin that is dealt with in our relationship with God, and that relationship cannot be broken. It is our "sins" that come into play regarding our ongoing fellowship with Him.

When our daughter was young, she took piano lessons. When she would attempt to learn a new piece, she would make it through the first staff, and invariably about halfway through the second, she would make a mistake. She would start over, much louder, go all the way until she made the same mistake, at which time she would repeat the whole process again and again. How many times can you listen to "I Dropped My Dolly in the Dirt" without losing your sanity?

I thought about my daughter when writing this chapter. Her piano practicing reflects the way many of us attempt to live the Christian life. We have tried to start over a thousand times. I don't need a new and louder beginning. I already know the first five bars of the Christian life by heart. I need to keep going, to confess my sins and finish the song. True confession leads to true forgiveness!

As you memorize this verse, meditate on the wonderful way God has made for us to live a life free from the sins of guilt that shackle so many. He dealt with our *sin* once and for all on the cross. He now deals with our *sins* by cleansing us in response to our continual confession. As God brings issues to your mind during times of devotion and meditation, agree with Him and live in the solid promise that is yours in 1 John 1:9: "He is faithful and just to forgive!"

23 THE GREAT COMMANDMENT

" 'You shall love the LORD your God with all your heart, with all your soul, with all your strength, and with all your mind,' and 'your neighbor as yourself.' "

LUKE 10:27

What is your primary purpose in life? Everything has a primary purpose. The primary purpose of an automobile is to transport us. I would rather have a Chevrolet that starts every time and got me where I needed to be than a fancy, shiny foreign car that only starts on occasion. The primary purpose of a pen is to write. I would rather have a cheap plastic one that writes well than a fancy German pen that skips and does not perform well. Our own primary purpose is found in the words of this week's verse: "love the LORD your God . . . and your neighbor as yourself."

All the commandments of God are pure, but only one is called "great." And it is the one dealing with love for God and for our fellow man. This commandment is called great because it includes all the Ten Commandments within one verse. The first four of "The Big Ten" have to do with our relationship with God (Exodus 20:2–11). Thus, Jesus said, "You shall love the LORD your God." The last six have to do with our relationship with one another (Exodus 20:12–17). Thus, our Lord continued, "And [love] 'your neighbor as yourself.'" The first half of the Great Commandment has to do with our attitude and the last half with our actions. Here again is the principle of *being* coming before *doing* that we see woven throughout the fabric of Scripture.

OUR ATTITUDE

"You shall love the LORD your God with all your heart, with all your soul, with all your strength, and with all your mind,"

The Lord Jesus referred to this as a commandment. It is not an option, nor is it a suggestion. And it is important to note that this commandment is directed to those who know Christ in a personal way through the new birth. It is the Lord *your* God to whom He referred. You cannot truly love someone unless you really know that person, and you cannot know someone unless you spend time alone with that person. The emphasis here is on loving the One who first loved us and gave Himself for us.

We are to hold nothing back when we love God. We are to love Him with all our heart. Jesus once spoke of those who honored Him with their lips but not their hearts—they were far from Him (Matthew 15:8). We are to love God with our entire mind. A heart full of love is no excuse for an empty mind. And our attitude should reveal that we love God with all of our strength and soul. In other words, our entire person is to be given over to God in love.

OUR ACTIONS
"[love] your neighbor as yourself."

If we truly have an attitude of love toward the Lord, then actions revealing our love for others around us will be as natural as water running downhill. This Great Commandment is given to us in the context of the story Jesus told of the good Samaritan. He concluded this story of love for others with an admonition to "go and do likewise" (Luke 10:37). Love is always equated with action. Love is something we do. If our attitude is wholehearted love for Christ, then our actions will result in love for those around us.

Jesus said we are to love our neighbors "as we love ourselves." Many who have not found their true identity in Christ have a real issue here. Many have little self-respect or self-love. This is why this commandment is directed to those who have fallen in love with the Lord Jesus, because only those of us who find our self-worth in Him can love on the level He commands.

Keeping things in proper order is vitally important. We are to love God first and foremost. When we do this, our actions toward others will issue out of a loving attitude for Him. This fact reveals the fallacy of humanism.

Humanism tells us just the reverse of what Jesus said in the Great Commandment. This world system tells us the way to love God is to love man first. But Jesus said, "No, the way to truly love your neighbor is to love the Lord supremely."

Years ago when I fell in love with my wife, Susie, we were separated by a couple of hundred miles. I was in school in Fort Worth, and she was in school in Austin. I quickly discovered that when two people fall in love, they like to be together. They like to be together . . . alone! They like to write each other letters or send e-mails. They like to talk daily on the telephone. Do you love God? A good test is to ask yourself these questions: Do I like to be with Him? Do I like to be with Him . . . alone? Do I enjoy reading His love letter to me, the Bible? Do I delight in talking to Him in prayer?

Yes, everything has a primary purpose. The real question is "Are we fulfilling God's primary purpose in our lives by obeying the greatest of all the commandments?"

As you memorize this verse, meditate on the fact that this commandment from the lips of our Lord is so powerful that, in this one verse, He put all the Ten Commandments: "Love the LORD . . . and . . . your neighbor as yourself."

24 THE NEW COMMANDMENT

"A new commandment I give to you, that you love one another; as I have loved you, that you also love one another."

JOHN 13:34

M y high school chemistry teacher used to always talk about the "acid test." The acid test is a sure-fire way to identify a substance. The Bible reveals that the acid test of the Christian life is love. Love is not simply a virtue of the Christian life; it *is* the Christian life. It is the oxygen of the kingdom. There is no life without it. Everything—the spiritual gifts, prophecy, knowledge, wisdom—will come to an end, but love knows no end. It goes right on through the portal of death and into eternity. Paul said that if we "have not love, it profits [us] nothing" (1 Corinthians 13:3).

In the previous chapter we memorized the Great Commandment. Now, on the very evening before His crucifixion, our Lord gave us a "new commandment" that supersedes the others not only in attitude, but also in action.

A NEW RULE *"A new commandment I give to you, that you love one another; as I have loved you"*

A casual reading of this text might tempt the reader to pass over two very important words. For one, this is a *commandment*. It is not a suggestion or a mere option. It has behind it all the authority of the Godhead. And it is a *new* commandment. Although the language of the New Testament reveals that this commandment is not new in time (God's love has been around forever), this commandment is new in its expression. It is fresh; it is the opposite of worn out.

Until now, on the very eve of the crucifixion, the best we could do was to live on the level of the old commandment." This old commandment is found in Leviticus 19:18 and referenced in the Great Commandment. That is, we are to love our neighbor as we love ourselves. This self-love is a love with limits. It is often conditional on such matters as time or conduct, situations or social standing. It can lend itself to selfishness because it speaks of a self-love. It can also be changeable and fickle.

But real love is expressed by a new rule. For thirty-three years Jesus gave us a picture of how real love was to be evidenced. Up until then, the best we could do was to live on the level of the old commandment of self-love. In essence, Jesus said, "For over three decades now I have shown you real love. I am about to leave you, so before I go, a new commandment I am giving you. No longer are you to love one another as you love yourself, but 'as I have loved you.'"

A NATURAL REACTION
"as I have loved you, that you also love one another."

We are totally incapable of loving like this on our own. The only way this can become a natural reaction for us is to experientially know the love of Christ in our own hearts. This new commandment changes things. No longer are we to love on that self level. Now, we are to love as Jesus loved us—unconditionally. Once we receive His love, we are to release it to others in the same way He loves us. Talk about revolutionary thinking, here it is personified.

In order to love others on this level, we must know the kind of love Jesus loves us with. His love is *unlimited*. Paul said to the Romans that nothing "shall be able to separate us from the love of God which is in Christ Jesus our Lord" (Romans 8:39). To the Ephesians, he expressed it as the "width and length and depth and height" of God's love (3:18). Not only is Christ's love to us unlimited, but it is also *unconditional*. It is not conditioned upon time or conduct or situations that may be in play. In fact, "God demonstrates His own love toward us, in that while we were still sinners, Christ died for us" (Romans 5:8). His love is also *unselfish*, so much so that it took Him all the way to the cross. And of course, we should note that His love is also *unchangeable*.

As the writer of the Hebrews said, "Jesus Christ is the same yesterday, today, and forever" (13:8). Thus, as we beat out our love relationships on the anvil of our own personal experience, we will love others with a love that is unlimited, unconditional, unselfish, and unchangeable. That is, if we love others as Jesus has loved us.

What is the result of this type of love? The very next verse is explicit: "By this all will know that you are My disciples, if you have love for one another" (John 13:35). Perhaps John put it best when he said, "Beloved, let us love one another, for love is of God; and everyone who loves is born of God and knows God. He who does not love does not know God, for God is love" (1 John 4:7–8). This longtime recipient of Christ's love added, "We know that we have passed from death unto life, because we love the brethren" (1 John 3:14).

Yes, love *is* the Christian life. It is the oxygen of the kingdom. It is the acid test of our own discipleship. God did not write in the sky or send a tract in order to reveal His love toward us. He sent His Son. Love did that. He demonstrated His love to us.

As you memorize this verse, meditate on the fact that the Bible reveals a picture of real love to us in everything Jesus said and did. Our challenge is now to obey the "new commandment" by loving others on this higher level of love, in the same way that Jesus loves us.

25 THREE VERSES FOR YOUTH . . . AND THE REST OF US!

Therefore, whether you eat or drink,
or whatever you do, do all to the glory of God.

1 CORINTHIANS 10:31

❖❖❖❖❖❖❖❖❖❖❖❖❖

*S*hortly after I became a follower of Christ at age seventeen, someone told me three very important verses for young believers to know. I distinctively remember immediately writing them in the flyleaf of my Bible. Over those first months of my Christian walk, only God knows how many times I referred to them until they were forever locked in the memory bank of my mind.

Over these almost five decades of Christian living, I have owned dozens of Bibles in all sizes, translations, colors, and languages. However, they all have one thing in common. These same three verses are found, written in my own hand, on the flyleaf of each one of them.

From time to time in our individual life journeys, we all come to temptation's corner, that place where we are called to make a decision as to which way we should turn. The tempter is always standing there in the intersection seeking to entice us to make a wrong turn. The three verses highlighted in this chapter reveal three very important, even crucial, questions we should ask ourselves as we anticipate which way to turn at one of these inevitable intersections of life. Let's look at them, learn from them, and write them in the flyleaf of our own Bibles.

CAN I THANK GOD FOR IT?

When we find ourselves at temptation's corner, we should ask ourselves, "If I go this way, say this thing, or do this deed, then when all is said and done, can I thank God for it?" The Bible says, "In everything give thanks; for this is the will of God in Christ Jesus for you" (1 Thessalonians 5:18).

We are called upon to give thanks "in everything." If there is some attitude or action on our part for which we could not give God thanks in the aftermath, then we should avoid it at all costs. Interestingly, we are not called upon to thank God *for* everything but *in* everything.

CAN I DO IT IN JESUS' NAME?

In Paul's letter to those at Colossae, he admonished the believers—and us—saying, "Whatever you do in word or deed, do all in the name of the Lord Jesus, giving thanks to God the Father through Him" (Colossians 3:17). We are not only to give thanks in all things, but we are to do all things in the name of the Lord Jesus as well.

Can you imagine what would happen in our life if we gave serious thought to this issue? It would make a huge difference in what came out of our mouths. It would make a huge difference in what we did. It would make a huge difference in what we watched and in what we read. Can I do it in Jesus' name? If we would ask ourselves that question when we stand at temptation's corner, a world of things we say and do might be different. There is one other question, and it finds its roots in our verse for this chapter.

CAN I DO IT FOR GOD'S GLORY?

The Bible says, "Therefore, whether you eat or drink, or whatever you do, do all to the glory of God" (1 Corinthians 10:31). The true believer is motivated by a desire to bring God glory in every facet of life. If we asked ourselves this important question more often, we would not do many of the things we do or say many of the things we say.

None of us is immune to temptation's corner. In fact, all of us arrive there every single day, several times a day, in one way or another. Stop. Don't just rush through the intersection or make a hasty wrong turn. Ask yourself three important questions: Can I thank God for it? Can I do it in Jesus' name? Can I do it for God's glory?

As I type this chapter on my computer, I am thanking

God for that unknown and forgotten individual who so long ago shared these vital verses with me. Keeping them in my mind and in my thoughts has saved me from many wrong turns that I have been tempted to make along the way. I have found out that they are not just verses for youth, but for all of us.

As you memorize this verse, meditate on the truth of God's Word: "In everything give thanks." "Whatever you do . . . do all in the name of the Lord Jesus." "Whatever you do, do all to the glory of God." And don't forget to ask yourself—*Can I thank God for it? Can I do it in Jesus' name? Can I do it for God's glory?*

26 THE HEART OF
THE MATTER

*"For the LORD does not see as man sees; for man looks at the
outward appearance, but the LORD looks at the heart."*

1 SAMUEL 16:7

*W*hen the prophet Samuel went to Bethlehem to
anoint the future king of Israel, he sought out a son
of Jesse. The proud father lined up his six strong and strap-
ping, hardened and handsome sons before the prophet.
They were the personification of the best the flesh had to
offer. However, Samuel was not impressed. He inquired
if there was not another son. Indeed there was. He was a
"ruddy" shepherd boy named David who was out tending
his father's sheep. The rest is history, and Samuel reminded
us that "man looks at the outward appearance, but the
LORD looks at the heart." The Lord looks where? At the
heart.

Now to the heart of the matter. What is it, exactly, that
the Bible refers to when it mentions "the heart"? The word
appears over eight hundred times in the King James Version. Is it that mass of muscle, about the size of a man's

fist, located in front of his vertebral column and in back of his sternum? Is it that organ that beats, on average, about seventy-two times a minute or, in the course of a day, over one hundred thousand times—and, for the most part, without our conscious awareness? Is it that mass of muscle that beats 28 million times in a year and, if we reach age seventy, will have beaten steadily 2.5 billion times?

One of the helpful principles in understanding biblical truth is what might be called the "law of first mention." That is, there is significant insight to be found as to the meaning of a word by studying its first uses in Scripture. In the early chapters of Genesis, we see three clues that reveal to us what God's Word really means when it refers to the heart.

THE HEART IS OUR INTELLECT

"Then the Lord saw that the wickedness of man was great in the earth, and that every intent of the thoughts of his heart was only evil continually." (Genesis 6:5)

This is the first use of the word *heart* in the Bible. Here, it is associated with the thought process, the intellect. When the Bible speaks of the heart, it is not referring to the actual physical organ that pumps blood throughout our circulatory system, but to the thoughts that help shape our being. This is why we read, "As he thinks in his heart, so is he" (Proverbs 23:7). The heart is our intellect, the thinking part of our being.

When we read that the Lord looks upon our heart, we

understand that He is watching how we think, whether our thoughts are pure or not. Yes, while man can only observe our outward appearance, the Lord has the capacity to look into our hearts, to know what we really think.

THE HEART IS OUR EMOTIONS
"[The Lord] was grieved in His heart." (Genesis 6:6)

The second occurrence of the word *heart* in Scripture reveals that it involves our emotions. When the Lord saw the rebellion of man, it "grieved [Him] in His heart." The heart is the seat of our emotions. It is not simply our intellect; it involves our feelings as well. How many thousands of love songs have been written about the heart?

When the good Samaritan saw the beaten man on the road to Jericho, the Bible reveals that "he had compassion" upon him. Another translation says, "His heart went out to him" (Luke 10:33 MSG). The night before the crucifixion, with His disciples in Gethsemane's garden, the Lord revealed that "My soul (heart) is exceedingly sorrowful, even to death" (Matthew 26:38). And we have Solomon's reminder that "a merry heart does good, like medicine" (Proverbs 17:22). Compassion, grief, sorrow, and happiness are all emotions that emanate from the heart. When the Scriptures speak of the heart, they are speaking to us of our intellect and our emotions.

THE HEART IS OUR VOLITION

*"Then the L*ORD *said in His heart, 'I will.'" (Genesis 8:21)*

This third appearance of the word *heart* refers to the essence of our own will, our volition. The Lord said "in His heart, 'I will.'" Often we find this volition entwined with the heart. The prodigal son was out in the far country, a long way from home, when his heart was changed. He changed his mind. Or, as the Scripture says, "he came to himself" (Luke 15:17). Once this happened, he changed his volition. He said, "I will arise and go to my father" (v. 18). Then he got up and turned his heart—his intellect, his emotion, his volition—toward home.

It is God Himself, at our conversion, who takes that old heart of ours and gives us one that is brand-new. For He said, "I will give them a heart to know Me, that I am the LORD; and they shall be My people, and I will be their God, for they shall return to Me with their whole heart" (Jeremiah 24:7).

As you memorize this verse, meditate on the truth that, while man may look on the outward appearance, God is looking upon our hearts. He is mindful of our thoughts, our emotions, and our will. Today is a good time to "return to the LORD with all your hearts" (1 Samuel 7:3). And that is the real heart of the matter.

27 FINDING THE WILL OF GOD

"Father, if it is Your will, take this cup away from Me;
nevertheless not My will, but Yours, be done."

LUKE 22:42

s the shadows fall upon Gethsemane, we find our Lord so anguished in prayer that He began to literally sweat drops of blood. His passion was to accomplish the Father's will for His life. Earlier, He had pointedly addressed this with His disciples by saying, "I have come down from heaven, not to do My own will, but the will of Him who sent Me" (John 6:38). Now, on the evening before He would hang on a Roman cross bearing the weight of the sins of the world—it was this desire that consumed Him. That is, "Not My will, but Yours, be done."

God has a purpose and a plan for each of His children. King David revealed his confidence that God would not conceal His will when he declared, "You will show me the path of life; in Your presence is fullness of joy; at Your right hand are pleasures forevermore" (Psalm 16:11). The Lord Jesus is more interested in us finding His will for our lives than we ourselves are.

On certain issues God's will is quite straightforward. For example, Jesus said, "This is the will of Him who sent Me, that everyone who sees the Son and believes in Him may have everlasting life" (John 6:40). There is no doubt that those who believe in Christ will have everlasting life. This is the explicit will of the Father. But what about other issues of life, other crossroads that come our way, demanding our attention and an eventual decision? How do we go about the business of finding out what is really God's will for us instead of what may simply be a selfish, personal desire? There are some important steps we can take along the way toward finding God's will.

BE SURE YOU KNOW THE SAVIOR

It stands to reason that if we are on a pursuit to find God's will in a certain area, first of all we have to come to know Him as our very own personal Savior. Paul made this crystal clear in his first letter to his apprentice Timothy, "For [leading a quiet and peaceable life in all godliness and reverence] is good and acceptable in the sight of God our Savior, who desires all men to be saved and to come to the knowledge of the truth" (1 Timothy 2:3–4).

The initial step in finding God's will is to be sure you know the Savior. Without a saving knowledge of Christ and His abiding life within, a person cannot discern the things of God. These things are, as Scripture says, "spiritually discerned" (1 Corinthians 2:14).

BE SURE YOU KNOW THE SPIRIT

Once we place our trust in Christ, the Holy Spirit comes to take up residency within us, empowering us for service, helping us "bear witness" with the Spirit of God. Paul admonished us to "not be unwise, but understand what the will of the Lord is. And do not be drunk with wine . . . but be filled with the Spirit" (Ephesians 5:17–18). When we know Christ as Savior and are being controlled by His Spirit, He becomes our Teacher and will "guide [us] into all truth" (John 16:13). Being sensitive to the Spirit's leading in our lives is a key factor in discerning God's will for us.

BE SURE YOU KNOW THE SCRIPTURE

When we want to find God's will, it is essential that we have knowledge of biblical truth. God will never lead one of His followers to do anything that is contrary to the Scriptures. Paul's challenge to us was therefore to "let the word of Christ dwell in you richly in all wisdom" (Colossians 3:16). When we know Christ, when we are being controlled by His Spirit, and when we are abiding in His Word, He "will make known to [us] the path of life" (Psalm 16:11 NASB).

Along with these three supernatural phenomena, there are three practical ways to find God's will. The first key word is *desire.* God will not call you to a certain endeavor without first planting a desire within your heart to do that very thing (see Psalm 37:4). For the person who is abiding in the Spirit and in the Scripture, the desires of the heart are implanted by God Himself. He gives the desires that are in our hearts. The second operative word is *opportunity*. Just because we have a desire does not necessarily mean it is God's will for us. If it is God's will, the desire will be accompanied by an opportunity. Third, we are to keep walking and trust that, if this path or our destination is not God's will, He will shut the door.

This is exactly what happened on Paul's second missionary journey. He had a desire and opportunity to go to Asia and Bithynia. But on each occasion God shut the door: "the Spirit did not permit" Paul to go in (Acts 16:7). There was no rebuke. It was simply not God's will at the moment. Immediately after this, Paul heard God call him to Macedonia, and he went straight there, totally in the middle of the will of God. The Bible says, "After he had seen the vision, immediately we sought to go to Macedonia, concluding that the Lord had called us" (Acts 16:10). The word *concluding* means that it all came together. Paul sought and found the will of God, and the great revival at Philippi broke out as a result.

God does not want to veil His will from you. He is more desirous of your finding it and walking in it than you are yourself. Yes, He has a wonderful plan for your life, and He longs to make His will known to you.

As you memorize this verse, meditate on what knowing Christ means to you personally. Recall the day when you first placed your trust in Him and were born again. Meditate on what knowing the Spirit means as you yield to Him. And make time to meditate on the Scriptures for here we find His will so often written for us in black and white. Finally, join Jesus in praying, "Not my will . . . but Yours be done."

28 GOD'S ANSWER TO CULTURAL CHAOS

In Him we have redemption through His blood,
the forgiveness of sins, according to the riches of His grace.

EPHESIANS 1:7

*O*ur Western culture has seen a systematic and degenerative decline in traditional values over the past many decades. By and large, the American church has awakened to the reality that at least two generations have been lost to the church. Culture warriors and analysts of social trends have identified several common characteristics of these "lost generations."

Among the most prominent of these characteristics are five specific ones that rise to the surface. The number one quest of these lost individuals is a search for a *meaningful relationship* in life. Many have never known one. For the most part, they are the product of a culture of divorce, and they are crying out for a meaningful relationship. Second, they desire *immediate gratification*. "Give it to me now" is their cry. They have grown up in a world where everything is instant, especially with information on the Internet. Thus, they do not want to wait for anything. Next, they want *something for nothing*. People on both ends of the economic spectrum have an entitlement mentality. On one end, certain government entitlement programs have reinforced this compulsion. On the other end, wealthy parents have given their children every material need or want imaginable, and they have never had to work for anything. Fourth, these lost generations want *guilt-free living*. But at night, when they turn the light off, they still have a conscience that longs for some moment to be lived over again. Finally, they are on a *search for prosperity*, but they have little hope of obtaining it. They will be the first generation in American history that, on the whole, will not raise their children in homes as nice as the ones in which they were raised.

Who has the answers that meet the needs and desires of these younger generations? Ironically, only the church holds the answers and can meet all five needs of these lost generations. And all five are found in one single verse of Scripture: Ephesians 1:7.

THE LORD OFFERS SOMETHING PERSONAL *"In Him"*

These young adults are on a quest for a meaningful relationship in life. Note the first two words of Ephesians 1:7: "in Him." What Christ has to offer is not about religion or ritual. It is about a relationship, a vibrant, personal relationship with Him. What He offers is "in Him." The very thing for which the lost generations are searching is only found in Christ. The bottom line is, we will never be properly related to others until we are properly related to ourselves. And we will never be properly related to ourselves until we discover how valuable we are to Christ and enter into a personal relationship with Him. Christ is the only One who has the answer for the very thing that compels our search for significance—a meaningful relationship in life.

THE LORD OFFERS SOMETHING PRESENT *"we have redemption"*

The second characteristic of these lost generations is a search for immediate gratification. Note the second phrase in our text: "we have redemption." What Christ has to offer is for right now. This tense is present active indicative, meaning the event is occurring in actual time right now. While they may think all Christ has to offer is for some future life in heaven, the reality is that He makes a difference right now. The day when, as a seventeen-year-old young man, I came to know Him, I was overwhelmed with the reality that He made an immediate difference in me: "Christ *in me*." Talk about immediate gratification! I found it that day. It is only found in knowing Him.

THE LORD OFFERS SOMETHING THAT'S PROVIDED *"through His blood"*

What Christ has to offer is free. He provides it without cost or condition. He is the very thing for which these young adults are searching. And we who know Jesus are the only ones who have the answer to their hearts' deepest needs. It is not by His power or His love or His teaching, but by His blood that He has purchased a way for us to be in relationship with the Father. That privilege is neither earned nor deserved and cannot be bought. It is provided freely to us through the sacrifice of Jesus' blood.

THE LORD OFFERS SOMETHING PROFITABLE *"the forgiveness of sins"*

These young people lost to the church are also searching for guilt-free living. Again, we who know Jesus are the only ones who hold the answer to their hearts' desires. Only through Christ can we find forgiveness for sins through our confession. Then, as the psalmist promises, "As far as the east is from the west, so far has He removed our transgressions from us" (Psalm 103:12). Aren't we glad he said the east from the west instead of the north from the south? The north and south have an end. There is the North Pole and the South Pole. However, the east and west know no end; they simply keep going. God removes our sin from us forever.

THE LORD OFFERS SOMETHING
PURPOSEFUL *"according to the riches of His grace."*

Here we find the real answer to the quest for prosperity. Christ does not say *out of* His riches, but *according to* His riches. Let me explain. If I were to give you a dollar, I would be giving you *out of* my riches. But if I were to hand you a blank check with my signature affixed for you to use as you will, I would be giving to you *according to* my riches. God offers us His grace *according to* His rich supply. God is rich in His grace and mercy toward us. Yes, "for you know the grace of our Lord Jesus Christ, that though He was rich, for your sakes He became poor, that you through His poverty might become rich" (2 Corinthians 8:9).

What are we saying in this chapter? That the *something* people think they need is really *Someone*. And His sweet name is the Lord Jesus. He holds the answer to every need of every heart. Those answers are in Him and in Him alone.

As you memorize this verse, meditate on each of these five phrases and ask God to meet the needs of your heart at the very points of your personal needs. After all, "in Him . . . we have redemption . . . through His blood . . . the forgiveness of sins . . . according to the riches of His grace."

29 JESUS: THE ONLY WAY?

"I am the way, the truth, and the life.
No one comes to the Father except through Me."

JOHN 14:6

*T*his is the most exclusive statement to ever come from the lips of our Lord. He emphatically declared that He is the one and only way to eternal life, the door through which we all must enter. Without Him there is no "way," there is no ultimate "truth," and there is no real eternal "life." And if that declaration were not enough, Jesus went on to say that there is no way to get to the Father unless we come through Him. In a world where pluralistic persuasions are running rampant, the question arises today: Is Jesus Christ really *the* only way, or is He simply one of many ways to life eternal?

It has been noted by others in the past that leaders are often characterized by certain punctuation marks. Some think leaders should be characterized by the period, representing the command, the imperative: "Go here or go there; do this or do that." Some seem to think a leader is one who just issues commands and barks orders. Others assume that leaders should be characterized by the exclamation mark, symbolizing . . . enthusiasm! Expectancy! Optimism! In other words, this is the ability to motivate a crowd and instill an air of excitement among the followers. But more often than not, true leaders are characterized by the question mark. As someone has said, "That symbol is bent in humility."

The Lord was always asking questions. In fact, the Gospels record more than one hundred questions of His. One day at Caesarea Philippi, for instance, Jesus got to the heart of His exclusive claim by asking His followers two very pertinent and penetrating questions.

THE QUESTION OF PUBLIC CONSENSUS

Jesus asked, "Who do men say that I, the Son of Man, am?" (Matthew 16:13). This is the question of public consensus. In other words, what does the polling data indicate? Many people refrain from leading and decision making until they get the pulse of what the people want, not necessarily what they need. The disciples had just come from several days in Galilee where huge crowds had thronged to both the shoreline and the mountainsides to see and hear the Lord Jesus. They had been immersed in the Galilean crowds. They had their own polling data. So Jesus inquired about the consensus of the people: Who did they think He really was?

Many today never seem to be able to get out of this verse. They simply live in a world that is much more interested in what men say than in what God says. When our Lord asked this question, He was probing, seeking to open their eyes. The answers flew back in rapid succession: "Some say You're John the Baptist, others say Elijah, still others think You are Jeremiah, and others suggest You are just another one of the many prophets who have come our way" (Matthew 6:14). Unfortunately, things haven't changed much. We still live in a world that seems to be far more interested in what men say about Jesus than in what God says.

THE QUESTION OF PERSONAL CONVICTION

Then the Lord got up close and personal. He asked another question: "But who do you say that I am?" (Matthew 16:15). Do you see it? This is the question of personal conviction: "What about you? You . . . and you only. You and you alone. You and no one else. Who do *you* say that I am?" This is the question with eternal ramifications. It is the question that each and every one of us must face. Is Jesus who He said He was—the way, the truth, the life? Is He the only way to the Father and to eternal life?

God bless Simon Peter! We are often quick to stand in

condemnation of his quick temper and his often boastful comments, not to mention his own fateful denial the night the Lord needed him most. But here, in this scene, Peter was inspired by the Spirit and, without hesitation, made his great confession: "You are *the* Christ, *the* Son of the living God" (Matthew 16:16, empahsis added). What motivated Simon Peter, who made this confession, to later die his own martyr's death by crucifixion upside down? Explaining to his executioners that he was not worthy to be crucified in the same manner as his Master, Peter made the strange request to be executed on the cross upside down. What motivated this? Did he give his life for pluralism, for the idea that there are many roads to heaven? Did Peter give his life for inclusivism, the idea that everyone is eventually covered by the Atonement? No! A thousand times, no! Peter gave his life because he insisted that Christ is the only way to eternal life.

The very nature of truth is narrow. Mathematical truth is narrow: two plus two always equals four, not three or five. That is pretty narrow. Scientific truth is narrow: water freezes at 32 degrees Fahrenheit, not 34 or 35 degrees. Geographical truth is narrow: I live in Texas, and we are bordered to the north by the Red River, not the Sabine River. Historical truth is narrow: John Wilkes Booth shot Abraham Lincoln in the Ford Theatre in Washington, DC. Booth did not stab Lincoln in the back in the Bowery in lower Manhattan. So why should we be surprised that theological truth is narrow? It is the nature of all truth. Jesus said, "Enter by the narrow gate; for wide is the gate and broad is the way that leads to destruction, and there are many who go in by it. Because narrow is the gate and difficult is the way which leads to life, and there are few who find it" (Matthew 7:13–14). All truth is narrow.

Jesus is the only way to the Father's house. Indeed, He—and He alone—is "the way, the truth, and the life." And no one comes to the Father's house unless they come through Jesus!

As you memorize this verse, meditate on how Christ is the way . . . how He is the truth . . . and how He is the life. Don't find yourself being more interested in what men say than in what God says. He is still asking today, "Who do *you* say that I am?"

30 KEEPING LIFE IN FOCUS

Brethren, I do not count myself to have apprehended; but one thing I do, forgetting those things which are behind and reaching forward to those things which are ahead, I press toward the goal for the prize of the upward call of God in Christ Jesus.

PHILIPPIANS 3:13–14

Focus. That single word holds the key for success in so many different endeavors of life. This was at the heart of Paul's own interest when he challenged us to "set our minds on things above" in the Colossian letter (3:2). It was also at the heart of his message to the Philippians when he said, "This one thing I do" (KJV).

The powerful Federal Express company, headquartered in Memphis, Tennessee, exploded into worldwide prominence by simply bringing focus to one thing—overnight deliveries. Southwest Airlines is one of the nation's leading air carriers today primarily because of its single focus on low-cost coach travel with on-time performance. And who could talk about the element of focus without mentioning the Starbucks coffee chain. When all other coffee shops were busy dispensing all types of food services,

Starbucks simply developed coffee shops with a focus on, of all things, coffee!

Focus is fundamental to spiritual success as well as business success. Keeping the main thing the main thing in the midst of a multitude of other things is always a challenge for a follower of the Lord Jesus Christ. One of the key elements to spiritual growth is the ability to obtain and then maintain focus in the Christian life. Focus will lead us to do four things.

FOCUS WILL PUT OUR PRIORITIES IN ORDER

Paul said, "This one thing I do" (Philippians 3:13 KJV). Not ten things, not five things, not even two things. But "this *one* thing I do." Focus helps us put our priorities in order. First, you define your goal, and then it begins to define you.

FOCUS WILL GIVE US A FORWARD MIND-SET

Too many of us today spend most of our time looking around us or, worse yet, looking behind us. Focus enables us to begin to see our glass half full instead of half empty. It gives us a forward mind-set. Paul went on to say that he was "reaching forward to those things which are ahead." Paul's focus led him to possess a wise forgetfulness about the past and enabled him to make sure his reach continued to exceed his grasp.

FOCUS WILL SET US ON THE SECOND MILE

Focus brings a passion to our work that instills within us a desire to do what is required—and then some. Paul said, "I press." This word *press* carries with it the idea of an intense endeavor, much like an avid hunter who is pursuing his prey. Paul was pressing because he had focus; he had "one thing" as the main priority in life.

FOCUS ENABLES US TO KNOW WHERE WE ARE GOING

One of the most valuable assets focus will bring to us is the ability to know where we are headed. Paul said he was pressing toward "the goal." This word is a translation of the Greek word *skopos*, from which we get our English word *scope*. Like the scope on a rifle, focus will enable us to get our goals and priorities in the crosshairs. Focus enables us to know where we are going and how we are going to get there. It keeps our priorities in the bull's-eye of our target.

Focus is the fountainhead of successful living. It helps us to begin our task with the end in mind. So what is your goal in Christian living? What is in the crosshairs of your scope? When we begin to focus on Christ alone, we find that He will put our priorities in order, He will give us a forward look, He will set us on the second mile, and He will let us clearly see the end from the beginning.

As you memorize this verse this week, meditate on Christ and on Him alone. Put Him in the crosshairs and do that "one thing" you do, for the glory of His name. Keep your life in focus by keeping Christ in the center of it.

31 APPROVED OR ASHAMED?

*Be diligent to present yourself approved to God,
a worker who does not need to be ashamed,
rightly dividing the word of truth.*

2 TIMOTHY 2:15

*O*ne of the great temptations of the busy believer is to stop studying the Bible. After all, throughout many years of the Christian life, most of us have heard hundreds of sermons, sat through a multitude of Bible classes, listened to countless CDs and tapes, read a library of Christian books, and listened continuously to Christian radio. And this is not to mention the countless Internet Web sites with sermons and Christian information at our fingertips. Modern believers find themselves with so many resources that it becomes easy to spend most of our time reading about the Bible and less and less time actually studying God's Word itself, systematically and consistently.

Paul admonished young Timothy—and us—at this point, saying, "Be diligent [study] to present yourself approved to God, a worker who does not need to be ashamed, rightly dividing the word of truth." In this single verse, there are four important truths to apply to our own study habits.

THE BELIEVER'S MANDATE

The King James Version translates this command "to be diligent" as the word *study*. We are to be diligent and zealous about the task of studying God's Word. Since reference is made later in the verse to "rightly dividing the word of truth," Paul was challenging all believers to take very seriously their personal study habits. The Bible is a miraculous book in which personal study never ends. Bible study is a lifetime endeavor for the committed believer. It is our assignment, our mandate from God.

THE BELIEVER'S MOTIVATION

What is it that should motivate believers to undertake a lifetime of studying the Scriptures? It is so that when we are presented before the Lord Jesus, we might be "approved" by Him. The discipline of study is a stewardship from God, and believers should be motivated by a passionate longing to please the Lord, to hear Him say, "Well done, good and faithful servant" (Matthew 25:21).

THE BELIEVER'S MANNER

What is the manner by which we should go about our task of Bible study? We are to be workers who do "not need to be ashamed." Study is hard work. Doing word studies is laborious. Getting out our work tools of commentaries, Bible dictionaries, and lexicons is labor intensive. We are reminded that we are to equip ourselves for "the work of ministry," as Paul mentioned to the Ephesians (4:12). Dedicated believers are to be workers who devote themselves to the wholehearted study of God's Word.

THE BELIEVER'S MESSAGE

All of this is to be done in order that we might "rightly [divide] the word of truth." We should approach the Bible with a deep reverence, even a fear that we might mishandle or misrepresent God's truth. We should take caution against using every paraphrase we might find in order to twist the truth to match our own way of thinking about a matter. We are to be about the business of "*rightly* dividing the word of truth." This is a serious assignment. The believer's message should always be centered in, and issue out of, God's holy Word.

Think about it: we are God's workers. We will either be approved or ashamed when we stand before Him. This is our high calling and awesome task: to "be diligent to present [ourselves] approved to God, [workers] who [do] not need to be ashamed, rightly dividing the word of truth."

As you memorize this verse, lay aside all the resources and other study aids, and meditate on the Word alone.

32 PRODUCTIVE PARENTING

Train up a child in the way he should go,
And when he is old he will not depart from it.

PROVERBS 22:6

How many parents have stood upon this verse during the troublesome times of dealing with wayward sons or daughters? There is no promise here that the child will never sow some wild oats. The promise is the child will eventually return home to the truth upon which he or she was raised. Of course, the operative word in all of this is the very first word of the verse—*train*. This promise is not for all parents with prodigals. This promise is for those who "train" their children during their formative years in proper conduct, with positive correction, and with personal counsel "in the way he should go."

There is no more powerful example of this truth than the old and often told story of the prodigal son found in Luke 15. The irony of this parable's title is that Jesus told the whole story not about the boy but about his dad. Here is a father who appears to leave center stage in the drama to his two sons, one in rebellion and the other in self-pity. But this familiar parable is really about the father. The story begins, "A certain man had two sons" (v. 11). The father is the subject of the sentence. Jesus put the father on center stage here, not the son. So let's look at that father and learn from him.

SEE HIM WITH AN OPEN HAND
SAYING, *"I release you" (Luke 15:11–13)*

This dad was wise enough to know that the way to keep his child was to open his hand and let him go. Here was a father who was prepared to stand by the truths he had poured into that boy since childhood. In fact, here is the truth of Proverbs 22:6 unfolding before us. Some parents hold on to their children so tight they lose them. This dad was wise enough to know there came a time when he had to open his hand and let his son go. In every generation, there are always some prodigals who choose to learn life's lessons the hard way.

SEE HIM WITH OPEN ARMS
SAYING, *"I receive you" (Luke 15:20–24)*

When the boy "came to himself" and headed home, the father saw him "when he was still a great way off" (Luke 15: 17, 20). The father ran to meet him with open arms of welcome. No pointed fingers, no "Where have you been?" and no "How could you have done this to your mother?" Just open arms. The boy came *walking* but the father went *running*. We are not talking here about a boy who came home with the same rebellious spirit he had had when he left home, now simply sorry he had gotten caught. Here was a boy truly repentant. And here is a faithful father receiving him with open arms.

SEE HIM WITH AN OPEN HEART
SAYING, *"I restore you" (Luke 15:25–32)*

The most notable characteristics of this model father are his presence and his transparency. He was there for his sons no matter what their problems were. The most valuable gift he gave them was his presence. When the festivities and homecoming party were at their peak, where was Dad? We find him outside with the wounded older brother assuring him of his love and support.

We all need to be parents like this one, a father with an open hand and with wisdom enough to know that the way to lose our kids is to hold them too tightly and that the way to ultimately keep them is to let them go when the time comes. We need to be parents with open arms, always ready to make a way for our children's new beginnings. And we need to be parents with open hearts that are both transparent and encouraging.

The real message of Jesus' story is that our heavenly

Father deals with us in the same way that this father dealt with his prodigal. God our Father has open *hands* toward us. We are not puppets; we are real people. And the love we voluntarily return to Him is indescribably valuable to Him. He too meets us with open *arms*. And never were those arms opened as wide as they were on the cross. Finally, God shows us His open *heart*. He opened it on Calvary for the whole world to see, and He invites us into His arms today.

Henry Wadsworth Longfellow said that the parable of the prodigal son is the greatest short story ever written, in the Bible and outside of it. This parable is a vivid portrayal of the deeper biblical truth, "Train up a child in the way he should go, and when he is old he will not depart from it."

As you memorize this verse, meditate on the loving and forgiving heart of our Lord and ask Him to put a heart like that in you. Open your hands, open your arms, and open your heart this week to those needy and hurting people around you.

33 THE JOSHUA CODE

This Book of the Law shall not depart from your mouth, but you shall meditate in it day and night, that you may observe to do according to all that is written in it. For then you will make your way prosperous, and then you will have good success.

JOSHUA 1:8

*S*uccess is not a four-letter word! God's will for us, like His will for Joshua, is that we have "good success." Nehemiah, the faithful layman, returned to Jerusalem to lead in the rebuilding of its broken walls, and Nehemiah had the promise, "The God of heaven will give [you] success" (Nehemiah 2:20 NIV). It is said of Joseph, "The LORD was with Joseph and he was a successful man" (Genesis 39:2). And, here in the Joshua Code, we are told that if we keep the Word of God in our minds and in our mouths, day and night, and put it into practice, we will have "good success." But the Lord does not define *success* like many in our world do today. For the believer, *success* can be defined as the ability to find the will of God for your life . . . and then doing it!

Now, as the Israelites stood on the banks of the Jordan after forty years of wilderness wanderings, God's main emphasis for them was His Word, this Book of the Law. As reflected in this verse, the Joshua Code incorporates three important issues.

THE JOSHUA CODE INVOLVES A CONSTANT PRACTICE

The challenge is to meditate on the Word of God both "day and night," and meeting that challenge involves constant practice. This verse is a high-water mark in discipleship. No one before had ever been instructed to receive orders from God through the words of a book. Abraham obeyed God's voice when he was called out of Ur of the Chaldees. He did not have a Bible. He did not have a book. Joseph received God's revelation through God-given dreams. Moses heard the voice of God speaking through a burning bush (Genesis 12:1, 4; 37:5–10; Exodus 3:2, respectively).

Now, as Joshua stood at the threshold of the promised land, Moses was dead. However, Moses had left Joshua the Books of the Law that he had received from God— Genesis, Exodus, Leviticus, Numbers, and Deuteronomy. Thus, Joshua was the first man to learn the Word of God in the same way that we learn: from the words of a book. Joshua was to keep it in his mouth and in his mind. The emphasis for Joshua— and for us—is upon making Bible study a constant practice.

We are to "meditate" on it. That is, we are to go over and over and over God's truth in our minds to deepen its impression on us and to set it in our hearts. The word *meditate* indicates that Scripture is to be like a tune that we cannot get out of our minds. It just permeates our thinking processes. Living out the Joshua Code involves constant practice.

THE JOSHUA CODE INCITES A COMPLETED PURPOSE

What is the purpose of keeping the Word in our mind and in our mouth? So that "you may observe to do according to all that is written in it." By keeping God's Word in our minds and speaking it with our mouths, we are enabled and empowered to do what it says, to apply it to our lives.

Reading the Bible gives us knowledge about God. Anyone can do that. Knowledge is simply the accumulation of facts. *Obeying* the Bible is what enables us to have a knowledge of God. Many of us obey the Word . . . partially. We seem to pick and choose on occasion what it is we will obey and what we will ignore. This call is to "do according to *all* that is written" in the Word of God. Our completed purpose, in the eyes of God, will be to move beyond simply reading and studying the Bible, to an act of obedience as we put these words into practice in our own experience.

THE JOSHUA CODE INVOKES A CONDITIONAL PROMISE

Note the important four-letter word *then*. When we obey the Word, *then* we will have "good success." And how do we do this? We do it through the constant practice of meditating on God's Word and keeping it in our hearts, letting it permeate our very being and so direct the thought processes of our minds that we speak it with our mouths at points of need. In the initial psalm, the psalmist indicated that his delight was found in the Law of the Lord and "in His law He meditates day and night" (Psalm 1:2). Thus, we then complete the purpose of not simply hearing the Word, but also doing it as we put it into practice through personal obedience.

Here is true success in life: to stay in the *Word* of God until we find the *will* of God so that we can *walk* in the ways of God. The Word. The will. The walk. The Joshua Code invites us to feed on the Bible because it reveals to us God's will for our lives. And success is the ability to first find the will of God for our lives . . . and then act upon it, do it! At the wedding feast in Cana, Mary, the mother of Jesus, gave us one of the most valuable lessons of life when she said, "Whatever [Jesus] says to you, do it" (John 2:5).

As you memorize this verse, meditate on it by reading it enough times to put the inflection on each and every word it contains . . . and then do what it says. And then? You will have "good success."

34 THE SECOND MILE

"Whoever compels you to go one mile, go with him two."

MATTHEW 5:41

The phrase *going the second mile* has found its way into our modern vernacular. Its roots are found all the way back in first-century Palestine. The Romans had conquered most of the Mediterranean world. One of the marvels of their conquest was a vast system of super highways that they had built for travel to and from their conquered territories. There were more than fifty thousand miles of these Roman roads throughout the Empire. At each single mile was a stone marker. These mile markers pointed directions, determined the distance to the next town as well as to Rome itself, and warned of dangers that might lie ahead. Hence the common phrase "All roads lead to Rome."

By law, a Roman citizen or soldier could compel a subject from one of the conquered lands to carry his backpack, or load, for him for one mile, but one mile only. As Jesus was preaching His Sermon on the Mount, I have often wondered if He inserted the reference about the second mile when He saw an object lesson unfolding before Him and His hearers. He said, "Whoever compels you to go one mile, go with him two." Can you imagine the bombshell this must have been as it fell upon the ears of those under Roman occupation who were listening to His sermon? Jesus called upon His hearers to do what was required of them—and then some.

What is it that separates some from others in athletics or education or business or the arts, or in any endeavor? It is their drive to do more than is expected or required. The second mile is a secret to success in life. When focusing on the second mile, many forget there are two miles in play here. The first is a mandated mile; the second is a miracle mile.

THERE IS A MANDATED MILE MOTIVATED BY LAW

This first mile is often ignored. In fact, I never remember hearing a sermon or reading an article about the first mile, only about the second. The first mile is required of us. The first mile is always the hardest. Ask the distance runner. The second wind never kicks in on the first mile. The truth is, it is not as easy to enjoy the things we have to do as it is to enjoy the things we want to do.

The Christian life has its own mandated mile that is motivated by God's law. It is tough to get started on the first mile. Ask any first-century Jew under Roman rule. The first mile interrupts your schedule when you are compelled to perform it. It causes you to swallow your own pride and bear an extra burden. Likewise, often the most difficult part of the Christian life is getting started on the first mile. This is true with almost everything in life, with exercise programs, dieting, and scores of other disciplines. Even Scripture memorization! In fact, many try to play leapfrog with Matthew 5:41. That is, they want to enjoy the little extras of the second mile, but they do not want to deal with the requirements of the first mile.

THERE IS A MIRACLE MILE MOTIVATED BY LOVE

It is this miracle mile that separates certain individuals from others. The second mile is only made possible by being obedient to the first mile. The second mile has a way of brightening our own road. Think about it. Imagine a first-century boy working at his trade. A Roman soldier comes by, calls to him, and demands that he carry his backpack for one mile down the road. Now, this command interrupts the lad's whole day and takes him away from his work. But he has no choice. However, this boy is a second miler. They approach the one-mile marker and instead of putting down the pack, spitting on the ground, and marching back home, he volunteers to go an extra mile with the soldier. Along the way, he pleasantly inquires about life in Rome. The soldier is baffled. I have often wondered if that Roman soldier at the cross who said, "Truly this was the Son of God," had had such an experience earlier with a second-mile follower of Christ (Matthew 27:54).

Someone who journeys on the miracle mile also has a way of lightening the load of those around them. One cannot travel the second mile without influencing others. It only takes one second miler in a home to change the entire environment. It only takes one second miler on a team or in the office to do the same. This miracle mile, the second mile, is motivated by the love of Christ.

Incidentally, the second mile is the mile our Lord Himself walked. He knows the road very well. It was love that took Him on the miracle mile to the cross. Oh, He journeyed the first mile. He stepped out of heaven and into human flesh. He walked the mandated mile that was motivated by the law. He kept every detail of the law. But He also went the second mile, motivated by His own love for us. He who made the stars with a spoken word and formed the universe, the One who formed and fashioned us with His own hands, said, "I love you, and I will walk with you." But we went our own way.

Then He said, "I will go the second mile." It took Him to the cross where He bore the weight, not of a Roman soldier's backpack, but of our own sin. And somebody told somebody, and somebody told somebody else, and somebody else told Johnny Keeton, and Johnny Keeton told me when I was seventeen years of age. I am not all I ought to be today, but I have never been the same since that day.

As you memorize this verse, meditate on what ways you can go the second mile today. It will brighten your road and lighten someone else's load. ❧

35 A NEW BEGINNING

Entreat me not to leave you,
Or to turn back from following after you;
For wherever you go, I will go;
And wherever you lodge, I will lodge;
Your people shall be my people,
and your God, my God.

RUTH 1:16

*G*od is always the God of newness. The Bible continually refers to the fact that it is never too late for a new beginning. To Isaiah, the Lord said, "Behold, I will do a new thing" (Isaiah 43:19). To Ezekiel He said, "I will give them one heart and I will put a new spirit within them" (Ezekiel 11:19). The author of Hebrews spoke of "a new and living way" (Hebrews 10:20). And in the Apocalypse, John reported, "He who sat on the throne said, 'Behold, I make all things new'" (Revelation 21:5).

The words of our text today have become immortal. When famine came to Bethlehem, Naomi, her husband, and their two sons fled and settled in Moab. In due time, her sons married Moabite women. The Moabites were a race that was born in incest and a people who observed a false religion that was the antithesis to their Jewish heritage. Later, Naomi's husband died, as did her sons. Left with her two daughters-in-law, Naomi, upon hearing that there was now bread in Bethlehem, set her face like a flint to return to the will of God for her life. She encouraged the two women to go back to their people and to their gods. Orpah kissed Naomi and went back. The other, Ruth, clung to Naomi, saying, "Entreat me not to leave you, or to turn back from following after you; for wherever you go, I will go; and wherever you lodge, I will lodge; your people shall be my people, and your God, my God." These now familiar words constitute the formula for us when new things come and we cling to Christ in such a manner. When personal renewal comes to our own heart, it brings several new things.

PERSONAL RENEWAL BRINGS A NEW DETERMINATION

When Ruth said, "Entreat me not to leave you," she was declaring that even though her sister-in-law, Orpah, had turned back, she, with a new determination, would cling to Naomi. Her mother-in-law had made sure Ruth knew the way would be hard. Back in Bethlehem, Ruth's past and future would be against her. Ruth's decision came when all influences were against her—Naomi's insistence she leave, Orpah's example, and the religion of her childhood, to name just a few. Yet Ruth was determined to do the right thing and follow Naomi.

When new things come to us, they can bring a new determination. We say to our Lord what Ruth said to Naomi, "Entreat me not to leave you, or to turn back from following after you."

PERSONAL RENEWAL BRINGS A NEW DIRECTION

Ruth continued, "For wherever you go, I will go." In other words, she was saying, "This will be my life's direction." She had never been that way before.

A new direction is always a telltale sign of genuine renewal. We begin to become interested in the things in which Jesus was interested. As Ruth was to Naomi, so shall we be to Christ when personal renewal fills our heart. This kind of relationship brings a new determination and a new direction. Christ becomes the way we follow. Yes, He makes all things new as we say to Him, "Wherever You go, I will go."

PERSONAL RENEWAL BRINGS A NEW DEPENDENCE

Next, Ruth declared, "Wherever you lodge, I will lodge." Ruth was declaring that she would trust Naomi to meet her basic needs. Ruth had no place to lay her head at night. However, her determination instilled in Naomi a new dependence on God.

Ruth would instill this dependence in her children and grandchildren. Later, in Bethlehem, she would meet and marry Boaz, the lord of the harvest. They would have a son named Obed, who would have a son named Jesse, who would have a son named David—the shepherd, the psalmist, the king. And David would later say, "I have been young, and now am old; yet I have not seen the righteous forsaken, nor his descendants begging bread" (Psalm 37:25). Obviously, Ruth instilled this dependence on God in her children and her children's children.

Ruth knew that home was in the middle of God's will. When personal renewal comes, it is accompanied by a new degree of trusting the Lord to meet our basic needs.

PERSONAL RENEWAL BRINGS A NEW DESIRE

"Your people shall be my people" was Ruth's next declaration. Following Naomi brought a new desire in Ruth to embrace Naomi's people as her own. She was saying, in essence, "There will be nothing between us." Ruth realized that if she took the God of the Bible to be her God, she would have to separate herself from the godless crowd of Moab amongst whom she had lived. It is impossible to fellowship with God and refuse to fellowship with His people.

When I began to follow Christ as a young man, it did not take me long to learn that if I was going with Him, I had to go with His people. To love the Lord is to love His people and to find our fellowship among them. Among all the new things He brings at the point of our salvation is a new desire to say to Him, "Your people shall be my people."

PERSONAL RENEWAL BRINGS A NEW DEVOTION

Then Ruth confessed to Naomi, "Your God shall be my God." She was saying, "I am not only taking your people as my people, but your God as my God." If you wish to see an Old Testament conversion, it is here. And what a decision it was! Ruth's past was against her. She was raised in a heathen family who worshipped false, immoral gods. Her present was against her. No wonder Naomi pleaded with Ruth to go back to her own people. Her own future was against her. In Bethlehem she would be an exile from all she had ever known.

Ruth was giving up all she knew to follow Naomi's God, yet all Ruth knew from this God was suffering and sorrow. But Ruth also knew Naomi, and when she watched Naomi repent and set her face as a flint toward the right path, Ruth found not only a new direction and desire, but also a new devotion. Personal renewal brings a new devotion to our lives.

PERSONAL RENEWAL BRINGS A NEW DEDICATION

The next verse continues: "Where you die, I will die, and there will I be buried" (Ruth 1:17). Ruth was saying not even death would separate Naomi and her. Ruth was not coming back, even if things did not turn out as she thought they should.

We need the same dedication in following Christ. It costs us our life. Ruth would eventually die, as we all do. But first she would marry Boaz, and today she lives on in history and in heaven as an example for us all.

Most of us know the story well. Ruth went home with Naomi. She became the bride of the wealthy landowner Boaz. She lived a beautiful existence, totally separated from her old life. The whole course of her life was determined by another person! What a wonderful picture of you and me when we truly say to Christ what Ruth said to Naomi: "Wherever you go, I will go; wherever you lodge, I will lodge; . . . Your people shall be my people, and your God, my God." Yes indeed, He has a way of making "all things new" (Revelation 21:5).

As you memorize this verse, meditate on the wonder of how many things Christ has made new in you.

36 BACK TO BASICS

"But you shall receive power when the Holy Spirit has come upon you; and you shall be witnesses to Me in Jerusalem, and in all Judea and Samaria, and to the end of the earth."

ACTS 1:8

⬥⬥⬥⬥⬥⬥⬥⬥⬥⬥⬥⬥⬥

Once, the legendary football coach Vince Lombardi and his Green Bay Packers lost a football game that they should have won handily. However, sloppy play and foolish mistakes led to their unanticipated defeat. The next day at practice, Lombardi gathered his team together. He reached into a bag and brought out a football. He then said, "This, gentlemen, is a football." It was, in his own indomitable way, a statement that it was time to get back to basics.

When Christ was about to leave His team and return to heaven, He left them—and us—with a challenge to be His witnesses not only at home but also to the very ends of the earth. A few days earlier, on a mountain in Galilee, He had left us the Great Commission: "All authority has been given to Me in heaven and on earth. Go therefore and make disciples of all the nations, baptizing them in the name of the Father and of the Son and of the Holy Spirit, teaching them to observe all things that I have commanded you; and lo, I am with you always, even to the end of the age" (Matthew 28:18–20). His commission to us was explicit: we are to make disciples by leading people to Christ. We are to mark these new disciples through baptism. And then we are to mature them by "teaching them to observe" all those things Christ commanded.

Immediately before His ascension back to heaven, Jesus stood on another mountain in Judea. There He reinforced this Great Commission by calling upon that small group to take His good news to whole nations, not simply to a few locals. It is a basic tenet of the Christian faith that we are all to be His witnesses to a lost and dying world around us. The call to evangelism, to sharing the good news of Christ, is one of the most basic callings of the New Testament. Since the last words of those who leave us are always intriguing and important, let's dissect this parting challenge from the lips of our Lord and seek to apply it to our lives.

THE *WHO* OF EVANGELISM

"But *you* shall . . . be witnesses to Me." This challenge to take the gospel to the world is one Jesus gives to all of us. Two verses earlier, the disciples had tried to sidetrack the issue by asking questions regarding when Jesus would return and restore the kingdom. But Jesus did not say, "You shall be My chart makers or date keepers, but My witnesses—all of you!" None of us is exempt from this basic element of Christian living; that is, to share the good news.

THE *WHAT* OF EVANGELISM

You shall receive what? Power! This is a great need of believers today. We all need power to live the Christian life. Perhaps the greatest difference between the first-century church and the twenty-first-century church is summarized in two words—*influence* and *power*. Today we pride ourselves on our influence. We seek to influence the decaying culture around us in various ways. But the early church did not even have enough influence to keep their leader Simon Peter out of prison. They were virtually void of influence with the civil and legal authorities. But the more important news is, they had enough power to pray him out of prison!

Jesus used a word for power from which we get our word *dynamite*. We need this power to be His witnesses. The book of Acts is the story of a group of men and women just like you and me who—despite all the bigotry and bias of the Roman-ruled world—went out from a little upper room to tell the story of a publicly executed Jew. They did so much with so little. How? They had a dynamite nature about them. They had received power from on high.

THE *WHEN* OF EVANGELISM

When did this power come upon the group of believers? When the Holy Spirit came upon them. There is no such thing as a Christian without power. When you receive

Christ, you have the Holy Spirit. He takes up residency in you. Thus, you have power.

Early in our married life, Susie and I had a new Chevrolet. Well, it was not exactly new, but it was new to us. One morning I went out into our driveway, got in the car, and turned the key; it would not start. Upon raising the hood, I discovered that during the night someone had stolen our car's battery. That beautiful car was rendered useless. It could not transport me anywhere without a battery to energize it. I think of that car when I read this verse. Many church members get all dressed up and are ready to go out and witness, but they never seem to get started. Why? We are in need of a power outside of ourselves to energize us.

THE *WHY* OF EVANGELISM

The Holy Spirit enables us to be witnesses. This is the very reason why we have power—to be His witnesses. There should be no such thing as a Christian who is not a witness. If we are saved, we have Christ. If we have Christ, we have the Holy Spirit. If we have the Holy Spirit, we have power. And if we have power, we will be Jesus' witnesses.

The Lord did not call any of us to be a judge sitting in condemnation of others around us. He did not call us to be the prosecuting attorney, pointing our fingers of accusation at others. He did not call us to be the defense attorney, seeking to find loopholes so others could get past the law. He did not call us to be the jury, weighing all sorts of evidence for and against someone else. He called us to simply tell others what we have seen and heard from first-hand experience. That is, to be His witnesses. We are not recruiters trying to get people to join our club. We are not to be salesmen trying to persuade others to buy our product. We are simply to be Jesus' witnesses.

People marvel that God entrusted His holy gospel to such common men and women, void of formal training. They were true witnesses. Incidentally, the word translated "witness" is the same word from which we get our English word *martyr*. These early believers were witnesses (martyrs) in the truest sense. Many of them lost their lives because of their uncompromising witness of Christ.

THE *WHERE* OF EVANGELISM

Jesus told us to take His good news across the city, across the country, across the continent, and, yes, across the entire cosmos. Here is total participation: all of us are to be witnesses. And here is total penetration: we are to go "to the end of the earth." The gospel will never find its final destination until it is shared with every person on the planet.

In thirty short years, those early believers fulfilled Acts 1:8. How? They were empowered by the Holy Spirit and, with singleness of purpose, witnessed His saving grace in Jerusalem (Acts 1–8), in Judea and Samaria (Acts 9–12), and to the end of their world (Acts 13–28). They did not play leapfrog with this commission. They did not pass hundreds of witnessing opportunities in their own city in order to go to the ends of the earth. They began at home, in Jerusalem.

Christ's gospel is to penetrate the whole world until every religion is confronted, every error exposed, and everyone receives a witness. It is a huge task. But think about those early believers. Their assignment seemed geographically impossible: most people still believed the world was flat. Their assignment appeared to be physically impossible. They had no air travel, radio, television, printing presses, Internet, or any of the modern means at their disposal for communicating the gospel. It seemed legally impossible: they were forbidden by the government authorities to speak in Jesus' name. And it seemed socially impossible; after all, who would really listen to these scrubby Galileans, so void of culture and class? Yet, people did listen. They were witnesses through the power of the Holy Spirit. They did so much with so little, and we seem to do so little with so much. The time has come for the modern church to get back to basics, to follow the early believers' example, and fulfill Acts 1:8 in our lifetime as well.

As you memorize this verse, meditate on the awesome power that resides within each of us who has placed our faith and trust in Jesus Christ alone. It would do us well to also memorize the Great Commission (Matthew 28:19–20). Then get back to the basics of being Jesus' witnesses by making disciples, marking them by baptism, and teaching them to observe all He has commanded.

37 GOOD NEWS AND BAD NEWS

*For the wages of sin is death, but the gift of God
is eternal life in Christ Jesus our Lord.*

ROMANS 6:23

*M*odern culture has been replete with a series of good news/bad news jokes. For example, there is the one about the pastor who stood up on Sunday and declared, "The good news is we have enough money here this morning to pay off the church debt and to build our new building." Then he added, "But the bad news is, it is still in your pockets!" Or there is the one where the church moderator said, "The good news is the deacons have voted to send a get-well card to our ill pastor. However, the bad news is the vote was 31–30!"

When we come to Romans 6:23, one of the most informative and inspirational verses in the Bible, we find some good news and some bad news. The bad news is that "the wages of sin is death." But the good news is that "the gift of God is eternal life in Christ Jesus our Lord."

THE BAD NEWS

There is some bad news in this verse: "the wages of sin is death." The Greek word for *sin* is best understood as "missing the mark." The word picture describes an archer who shoots his arrow at the target and misses the bull's-eye. We all find ourselves here as "all have sinned, and come short of the glory of God" (Romans 3:23 KJV). We have all missed the mark, and the bad news is that its cost, or wage, is death.

A wage is what we get for doing something. We work a certain number of hours, and our employer pays us an agreed-upon wage. It is something we have earned, something we deserve. It is something we have coming to us. The Bible says, "the wages of sin is death." It is strange how many men and women sin, thinking it is going to pay dividends of fun and pleasure. But Satan is a liar. Sin pays its wage all right, but its wage is death, which is separation from all that is good.

Payday is coming someday. That is the bad news. When we miss the mark, it costs us greatly.

THE GOOD NEWS

But the good news is this: "the gift of God is eternal life in Christ Jesus our Lord." It is a gift, a free gift that cannot be earned nor deserved. We all remember the excitement of opening gifts as children around the

Christmas tree. We did not have to pay for those gifts. We did nothing to earn them. We simply opened them and received them. A gift is the opposite of a wage. We earn and deserve our wages. We don't earn or deserve a gift. If we did, it would be a reward and not a gift.

How is this all possible? We still have to deal with the bad news. Jesus made the way possible for us by dealing with the bad news Himself. Two thousand years ago on a Roman cross outside the city walls of Jerusalem, Jesus took the bad news and became sin for us. Yes, the wages of sin is death, and He died our death on the cross, paying the penalty for our sin. He paid the price, so now we can finish the verse with this good news, "but the gift of God is eternal life in Christ Jesus our Lord." He made a way out of no way. Our part is to receive this God-provided and free gift by faith alone in Him.

What a difference there is in these two bits of news. The bad news is that sin is costly, and it has a wage attached to it. The good news is that eternal life is free. It is God's gift to us. And that is no joke!

As you memorize this verse, meditate on the incredible price that Jesus paid for your sin. When we were so undeserving, He made a way for us to receive the greatest gift ever given, "eternal life in Christ Jesus our Lord."

38 REMOVING THE FEAR OF DEATH

Yea, though I walk through the valley
of the shadow of death,
I will fear no evil;
For You are with me;
Your rod and Your staff,
they comfort me.

PSALM 23:4

eath is the single common denominator of all men. This fact is illustrated every day in the morning newspaper. The business section of the paper highlights only those who are successful in their vocational endeavors. The social section contains pictures and stories only related to the social elite. The sports section is filled with articles about those teams and individuals who excel in their athletic fields. Then we come to the obituary section. There, listed side by side in alphabetical order, are the rich and the poor, the known and the unknown, the prominent and the not so prominent. We are all equal in death. It is our common denominator.

A lot of voices and volumes today tell us how to live.

Motivational and self-help books flood the marketplace. But there is only one book that tells us how to die. And there is no one verse in that Book of books which is more pertinent to the subject than our verse today. Tradition tells us that King David penned these words about the "valley of the shadow" while sitting in the Judean wilderness between Jerusalem and Jericho. The spot is known today as Wadi Kelt. It is a long valley about four and a half miles in length, and its canyons run as much as fifteen hundred feet in depth. The sun casts a shadow over the canyon on the sheep trails across the way, which snake their way up, down, and through the rugged terrain. It was here that David said, "Yea, though I walk through the valley of the shadow of death." This one verse reveals three important facts about the appointment that awaits each and every one of us.

FACT #1: DEATH IS A SURE THING

Death is sure. It is certain. We deal with death in many ways. Some attempt to flee it. Some go to the extreme of cryonics, freezing their bodies in hopes that future medical breakthroughs can bring them back to life at some later date. Some forget it. They simply reject the idea, assuming it will somehow go away. Others fear it—and they live paralyzed lives with no hope or security in Christ. Then there are those, like David, who face death. These people realize their days are numbered, and that we all have an appointment with death.

Note carefully David's words: "I *walk* through the valley." He walked. He didn't run toward death. This is King David, not Dr. Kevorkian. He didn't crawl, as though he wanted to postpone it as long as possible. He was not dragged toward it. He simply walked. He knew death could not be avoided; it is a sure thing.

FACT #2: DEATH IS A SOJOURN

David indicated that he walked *through* the valley. It was not his final destination. It was only a temporary passage, a sojourn. He knew this road was not a dead end with no way out. He knew it was not a cul-de-sac that got him nowhere. For David—and for us—death is simply a sojourn. We do not walk in the valley. We do not stay there. We walk *through* the valley.

The story is told of a caterpillar crawling along a limb on its belly. Along comes a friend with a philosophical view that says, "Someday I believe we will no longer crawl around like this but we'll be able to fly and soar and feast on milk and honey." *How idealistic*, thought the caterpillar. Then one day came his inevitable appointment with death. So he was buried in a shroud called a cocoon and attached to a twig on a tree. By and by, when spring came, the grave burst open, and out of it emerged a magnificent creature with delicate sails called butterfly wings. With our superior intellect, we know this is the process of metamorphosis. But do we know as much about our own destinies? Death is a sure thing, but it is also only a sojourn. It is not our final destination.

FACT #3: DEATH IS A SHADOW

Solomon reminded us in his Proverbs that "every word of God is pure" (30:5). Note carefully what David said: "Yea, though I walk through the valley of the shadow of death." No believer in Christ ever walks through the valley of death, only the valley of the *shadow* of death. The Lord Jesus, though, walked through the valley of death. For three days and nights He walked that valley and then emerged from the empty tomb and said, "Behold . . . I have the keys of death and of Hades" (Revelation 1:18 NASB).

Thus, the believer only walks through the valley of the *shadow* of death. A shadow might horrify you, but it cannot harm you. And the only way you can have a shadow is to have a great light shining. David said he walked "through the valley of the shadow of death" because that is what we do with a shadow; we simply walk through it.

While death is a sure thing, it is only a sojourn through a shadow. It is, in a sense, stepping into the light. Jesus said, "I am the light of the world. He who follows Me shall not walk in darkness, but have the light of life" (John 8:12).

Is it any wonder David went on in this verse to exclaim, "I will fear no evil"? He knew death would be defeated; that although it was a sure thing, it was but a temporary sojourn through a shadow into the light. David could fear no evil because he knew the Lord was with him: "I will fear no evil; for You are with me!" Up until now in this great 23rd Psalm, David had been speaking in third person: "He makes me . . . He leads me . . . He restores me." But when it comes to the subject of death, David got very personal. All of a sudden in verse 4, he changed to second person: "You are with me . . . Your rod . . . Your staff . . . You prepare . . . You anoint." Death has its own way of making Christ more personal.

No wonder we too need fear no evil. Why? Because the Lord is with us, and He has conquered death, hell, and the grave. The apostle John got a glimpse of Jesus' glory from his lonely island called Patmos where he was exiled. Upon seeing the vision of the exalted Christ, John formed the best description he could with our limited vocabulary and said, "When I saw Him, I fell at his feet as dead. But He laid His right hand on me, saying to me, 'Do not be afraid; I am the First and the Last. I am He who lives, and was dead, and behold, I am alive forevermore. Amen. And I have the keys of Hades and of Death" (Revelation 1:17–18). Yes, "though I walk through the valley of the shadow of death, I will fear no evil; *for you are with me*."

As you memorize this verse, meditate on the fact that, through His own death and resurrection, the Lord Jesus made a way when there was no way for us. We need not fear death. We only walk through the valley of the shadow of death . . . and Jesus is with us!

39 A FAITH THAT WORKS

For as the body without the spirit is dead,
so faith without works is dead also.

JAMES 2:26

❧❧❧❧❧❧❧❧❧❧❧❧❧❧

*T*here has always been an ongoing controversy in ecclesiastical circles over the nature of our salvation. People tend to gravitate toward one of two extreme views. One view overemphasizes faith while forgetting works; the other overemphasizes works while forgetting faith. The former is referred to as "easy believism." Proponents of this viewpoint think one can say a simple "sinner's prayer" without any change of lifestyle, any prayer or Bible study, or any desire for spiritual things and still be saved because he or she "prayed the prayer." The latter is referred to as a "works salvation." Proponents of this approach seem to think one can earn salvation through good works.

This conflict between faith and works is as old as the church itself. The entire argument finds its roots in the second chapter of James and in particular here in James 2:26: "Faith without works is dead." All through Scripture, the emphasis is on the fact that salvation is wholly by grace through faith in Christ Jesus alone and "not of works, lest anyone should boast" (Ephesians 2:9). However, the Bible also teaches that true saving faith is always accompanied by fruit and will result in good works.

James revealed that a faith without fruit is a false faith (James 2:14–17), a futile faith (vv. 18–19), and a fatal faith (vv. 20–26). Many misunderstand the message of James. He was not talking about a faith *with* works, but a faith *that* works. And there is an eternity's worth of difference between the two.

The famous reformer Martin Luther became so frustrated with this conflict, he went so far as to refer to the epistle of James as "an epistle of straw." But, again, the point is not about a faith *with* works, but a faith *that* works!

On the surface it appears to some that the message of Paul and the message of James are in diametric opposition to one another. For example, James asked, "Was not Abraham our father justified by works when he offered Isaac his son on the altar?" (James 2:21). Paul countered, "If Abraham was justified by works, he has something to boast about, but not before God. For what does the Scripture say? 'Abraham believed God, and it was accounted to him for righteousness'" (Romans 4:2–3). However, in reality, the two do not contradict each other; in fact, they actually complement each other.

FAITH AND WORKS ACCORDING TO JAMES

Some have accused James of attempting to answer Paul in this passage. Since James wrote his letter in 48 AD and Paul did not write the Roman letter until at least 58 AD, this theory has no merit. James and Paul were coming at the same issue from different perspectives. Paul was writing to the Judaizers who were saying that one had to add works of the law to faith in order to receive salvation. Thus his emphasis was on faith alone as the basis for salvation. Paul was arguing for the primacy of faith. James, on the other hand, was writing to people who went to the other extreme. They claimed to have faith but, in reality, had only intellectual assent. Therefore, his emphasis was on what Jesus called the "fruit" of our faith. James was simply arguing for the evidence of faith.

FAITH AND WORKS ACCORDING TO PAUL

Paul consistently emphasized that no one enters God's kingdom except by faith and by faith alone. James was in agreement with him. He began his letter saying, "[God] chose to give us birth through the word of truth" (James 1:18 NIV). Here in the second chapter, James was simply reinforcing the point that good works are the natural response of true saving faith. He was not saying that works are the requirement *for* salvation, but that they are the result *of* our salvation.

"As the body without the spirit is dead, so faith without works is dead." It is not a faith *with* works at issue here, but a faith *that* works. Paul reminded us that "we are His workmanship, *created* in Christ Jesus *for good works*, which God prepared beforehand that we should walk in them" (Ephesians 2:10, emphasis added). We are saved by faith alone, but faith that saves is never alone.

As you memorize this verse, meditate on the relationship between faith and works. And remember, it is a faith *that* works that pleases God.

40 ULTIMATE LOVE

But God demonstrates His own love toward us,
in that while we were still sinners, Christ died for us.

ROMANS 5:8

❧❧❧❧❧❧❧❧❧❧❧❧❧

I was a young pastor, and it was a bitter cold winter afternoon. Snow and ice covered the windswept cemetery
as I stood with a young couple at the open grave of their
newborn baby. We wept and prayed, I read Scripture, I said a
few words of comfort, and we left. I went home that evening
and could not get that brokenhearted mother and father out
of my mind. They went home that same evening and began
to put away the baby crib in which that little package of love
had slept for the past several weeks. On impulse, I went into
our firstborn daughter's room, picked her up, and sat down
in the den. I wondered how I would have felt had I been
that other young dad who sat in his home a few blocks away.
What if God had taken my child? After all, she was just a few
days old and, at the time, didn't know me anymore than she
knew the man next door. I came to the conclusion that what
would have bothered me most was that she would never
have known, in this life, just how much her father loved her
and was willing to give himself for her.

And that is the tragic thing about living a life without Christ. Those who do not know Christ can never know how much the Father loves them. Our God demonstrated His love when we were least deserving. He did something: He gave us His only Son who "died for us." No wonder the Bible says, "Greater love has no one than this, than to lay down one's life for his friends" (John 15:13).

THE PROOF OF GOD'S LOVE

God proved His love toward us. How? It was not by writing His love in flaming letters across the sky nor by belting His strong voice from heaven expressing His love. The Bible says, "When the fullness of time had come, God sent forth His Son, born of a woman, born under the law" (Galatians 4:4). Jesus was not some sort of remedial action, a last-minute splint for a broken world when everything else had failed. The preparation God had done was staggering. He had raised up a Greek nation that took the Greek language across the known world so the gospel could spread without a language barrier. He raised up a Roman empire that built a road system of fifty thousand miles across the world so the gospel could move from country to country. Yes, it was in the "fullness of time" that Christ came (Galatians 4:4).

Each of us longs to be loved. And God loves us so much that He demonstrated "His own love toward us": He sent

His Son. No one on the earth has DNA like yours. No one has a thumbprint just like yours. You are an individual, loved by the Lord. And the love you can voluntarily return to Him is indescribably valuable to Him.

THE PHENOMENON OF GOD'S LOVE

The phenomenal thing about the love of God is that He expressed it to us not when we were perfect or deserving. He loved us "while we were still sinners." In fact, "scarcely for a righteous man will one die; yet perhaps for a good man someone would even dare to die. *But God* demonstrates His own love toward us in that *while we were still sinners* Christ died for us" (Romans 5:7–8, emphasis added). Those two little words *but God* make all the difference.

Jesus came and clothed Himself in human flesh. He came to where we are so that one day we could go to where He is. In other words, He came to earth so we could go to heaven. He was forsaken so that we might never be forsaken. As someone said, "The Son of God became the Son of Man in order that the sons of men could become the sons of God."

THE PRICE OF GOD'S LOVE

"Christ died for us." Let those words sink in for just a moment. He died your death so you could live His life. He took your sin so you could take His righteousness. "For God so loved the world that *He gave . . .*"(John 3:16). For thirty-three years, He gave. We must have embraced and loved Him for it. But did we love Him? We hated Him. We spit in His face. We beat Him with a leather strap until His back was a bloody pulp. We stripped Him naked and mocked Him. We put a scarlet robe on Him and smashed a crown of thorns on His brow. And then we laughed . . . and laughed . . . and laughed. Then we plucked His beard out with our hands (Isaiah 50:6); then laughed some more. Finally, we took His hands—those same hands that once had calmed storms, stroked children's heads, multiplied the loaves and fishes, formed the spittle for the blind man's eyes, and clasped themselves in prayer in the garden—and we nailed them fast to a cross. Then we took those same feet that had run errands of mercy for so many, that had walked on the sea, and we nailed them to a cross.

The price Jesus paid to "demonstrate" His love was great. Every lash of the whip, every sound of the hammer, was the voice of God saying, "I love sinners."

As I held my little daughter tightly that night, I thought, *I'd give the world to her if I could.* Then it occurred to me that God had said just the opposite. He had said, "I'll give My Son to the world." It isn't any wonder the songwriter of old said, "Oh, the love that drew salvation's plan. Oh, the grace that brought it down to man. Oh, the mighty gulf that God did span . . . *at Calvary.*"

As you memorize this verse, meditate on "the breadth and length and height and depth" of God's love for you personally (Ephesians 3:18 NASB). No one else has your DNA. You are an individual, indescribably loved by God. Let Him love you today.

41   FORSAKEN!

And about the ninth hour Jesus cried out with a loud voice,
saying, "Eli, Eli, lama sabachthani?" that is,
"My God, My God, why have You forsaken Me?"

MATTHEW 27:46

※※※※※※※※※※※※※※

*D*uring the intense struggle of the cross, our Lord spoke seven times as He hung suspended between heaven and earth. This was the strangest of all His cries: "My God, My God, why have You forsaken Me?" Was Jesus actually forsaken by the Father during His moments of agony? As the battle raged, Satan tried his best to entice Christ to give up, to give in, and to give out. On the cross the enemy sought to get Jesus to give up, to call legions of angels to set Him free. This was the spiritual battle. When His disciples deserted Him, Satan tempted Him to just give in. This was the soulish battle. During Jesus' trials and beatings before the cross, the devil sought to get our Lord to give up. This was the physical battle.

Many today know the haunting feeling of being forsaken. Some people have once stood at a wedding altar and heard their lover promise to never leave them nor forsake them. But that didn't prove true, and now they know the painful reality of being forsaken. Countless children who have been abandoned by fathers and mothers also know the meaning of the word. Perhaps there is no more haunting word in our English language than the word *forsaken*. Let's take a brief journey with our Lord from Galilee to Gethsemane to Golgotha and learn from Him how to overcome being forsaken.

IN GALILEE JESUS WAS FORSAKEN BY HIS FAMILY *(Matthew 13:53–58)*

Jesus' own brothers and sisters distanced themselves from Him when He began His public ministry. They thought for a while that He was mentally imbalanced. It was at this point that He said, "A prophet is not without honor except in his own country and in his own house" (Matthew 13:57). Jesus had no honor "in His own house": He was forsaken by His family.

But when those who knew Him best forsook Him, instead of giving up . . . Jesus reached up. We read these words: "When He had sent the multitudes away, He went up on the mountain by Himself to pray. Now when evening came, He was alone there" (Matthew 14:23). When Jesus was forsaken by His own family, He did not give up. All alone, He reached up to His heavenly Father. This is a challenge for all of us who know the haunting reality of being forsaken. Instead of giving up, we can reach up to the Lord in prayer. He is the only One who can truly identify with your feelings and needs. For He too knows what it is to be forsaken.

AT GETHSEMANE JESUS WAS FORSAKEN BY HIS FRIENDS
(Matthew 26:36–56)

That night, before the Crucifixion, Jesus needed His friends and followers more than He ever had. But immediately after He had agonized in prayer, sweating drops of blood in Gethsemane's garden, the Bible bluntly states, "All the disciples forsook Him and fled" (Matthew 26:56). They forsook Him. And that is not all. They fled! They ran away. They denied they had ever known Him. They fled into the darkness of the night. Jesus was forsaken, abandoned, in His hour of deepest need. And He was forsaken not by His foes but by His own friends.

But after His disciples deserted Him, instead of giving in . . . Jesus reached in. Hear Him from under the olive trees of Gethsemane: "My soul is exceedingly sorrowful, even to death. . . . If it is possible, let this cup pass from Me; nevertheless, not as I will, but as You will" (Matthew 26:38–39). Our Lord did not give in to the circumstances that swirled around Him. Instead He reached in—into the depths of His own being to find His solace not in His own will but in the will of the One who sent Him. Have you reached in lately? That is, have you come to the place in your own experience where you join Jesus in praying, "Not as I will, but as You will"?

AT GOLGOTHA JESUS WAS FORSAKEN BY HIS FATHER
(Matthew 27:33–46)

What happened to compel Jesus to ask, "My God, My God, why have You forsaken Me?" For hours He had hung on the cross. Then darkness covered the land at noonday. There was a deathly silence. Then a cry penetrated the darkness: "My God, why have You forsaken Me?"

Does a loving God forsake His own? He did not forsake Daniel in the lions' den (Daniel 6). He did not forsake the three Hebrews in the fiery furnace of Babylon (Daniel 3). So why this strange cry from the lips of our Lord in His most agonizing moment? The Bible tells us that a holy God cannot look upon sin (Habakkuk 1:13). On the cross Jesus was bearing your sin and mine in His own body, suffering the punishment for our sins as though they were His own. As Isaiah said, "All we like sheep have gone astray; we have turned, every one, to his own way; and the LORD has laid on Him the iniquity of us all" (53:6). As Paul reminded us, "For [God] made [Jesus] who knew no sin to be sin for us, that we might become the righteousness of God in Him" (2 Corinthians 5:21). During the darkness, the Light turned away. There, on the cross, bearing our sin, Jesus was momentarily forsaken in order that we might never be forsaken.

When this happened our Lord was tempted by the devil to give out, to cry, "Enough! I quit!" But instead of giving out . . . He reached out. Hear Jesus from the cross as He reached out and said, "Father, forgive them, for they do not know what they do" (Luke 23:34). Hear Him reaching out to the dying thief alongside Him: "Today you will be with Me in Paradise" (v. 43). Jesus' arms are open wide to us today. And never were they opened wider than when they were stretched out on the cross. Jesus did not give out; He reached out.

What about your own life journey? Have you been to Galilee or are you there now, in that place where you are so tempted to give up? Reach up. This is the place where you surrender your will to His will. Have you been to Gethsemane or are you there now, in that place where you are so tempted to give in? Reach in. This is the place where you search yourself. Have you been to Golgotha, or are you there now, in that place where you are tempted to simply give out? Reach out. This is the place where you sacrifice your will to Him, as Christ did.

Yes, our Lord was forsaken by His family, His friends, and His heavenly Father—but only so we might never be forsaken. "Surely He has borne our griefs and carried our sorrows" (Isaiah 53:4). What a Savior!

As you memorize this verse, meditate on the way we never experience anything in this life that Jesus Himself did not experience before us and for us. Forsaken? Don't give up; reach up. Don't give in; reach in. And don't give out; reach out.

42   AMBASSADORS FOR CHRIST

We are ambassadors for Christ, as though God were pleading through us: we implore you on Christ's behalf, be reconciled to God.

2 CORINTHIANS 5:20

As believers, we have momentous responsibilities and assignments. We are to be ambassadors for the King of all kings. What exactly is an ambassador? An ambassador is a representative. For instance, the president of the United States will appoint an ambassador to represent the interests of our country in a particular nation somewhere in the world. Since the leader of our nation cannot be everywhere, he sends ambassadors to live in each of the various countries and represent the United States.

Paul said, "We are ambassadors for Christ." We are sent from heaven into this foreign land called Earth to be His representatives. We are to be Christ's ambassadors on our block, in our school, at our office, and wherever we may go. In order to truly represent our King with honor and integrity, we should know some of the common marks of an ambassador.

AN AMBASSADOR'S CITIZENSHIP

To begin with, it should be obvious that an ambassador from the United States to a foreign nation must be a citizen of America. No alien could ever represent our nation in a distant country. None of us would expect our government to, for instance, send someone from Syria to represent the United States in Egypt.

A true ambassador of Christ is one whose "citizenship is in heaven" (Philippians 3:20). Exiled on the island of Patmos, John said, "I . . . was on the island that is called Patmos . . . I was in the Spirit on the Lord's Day" (Revelation 1:9–10). John knew it was not where he was but *whose* he was that mattered most as he represented his Lord. Those who are truly Christ's ambassadors are those who have passed "from death to life" (1 John 3:14) and from darkness into light by trusting in Christ alone by faith for their salvation (1 Peter 2:9). Hence, they may reside "in the world" but they are not "of the world" (John 17:13–17). They belong to another kingdom.

AN AMBASSADOR'S CHARACTER

Representatives from the United States must be above reproach in character. Before they are ever appointed, they undergo the closest scrutiny imaginable. Their moral character, their financial dealings, their work record, their every word and deed come under the microscope. Ambassadors should be blameless in character.

Should ambassadors for the King of kings and the Lord

of lords be any less? As representatives of Christ, we should possess the highest moral qualities. Our reputation should be spotless and our character beyond reproach.

AN AMBASSADOR'S CONDUCT

Ambassadors must not have divided loyalties or interests. They must be selfless in their approach to representing their country. One who represents our country abroad must put in abeyance any conflict that might interfere with this assignment in any way. Their conduct must meet the highest moral standards if they are to effectively represent the needs and concerns of their nation.

The same certainly holds true for those of us who are ambassadors for Christ. It was on this point that the apostle Paul said, "He died for all, that those who live should live no longer for themselves, but for Him who died for them and rose again" (2 Corinthians 5:15). Christ expects those of us who represent Him in our world to live for Him with conduct that becomes our office.

AN AMBASSADOR'S CONSISTENCY

Ambassadors must be steadfast and live with unquestioned, consistent loyalty to their homeland. We would not want to have a US ambassador to Russia who could not be trusted. Ambassadors must be consistent in their dealings with, and totally loyal to, their government. If not, their actions would be treasonous.

I wonder if there are some ambassadors for Christ who should be tried for treason. Jesus saved us. He made us His own ambassadors, yet some of us have sided with the world's crowd. We seldom speak to others of Jesus' goodness nor represent His interests well. God desires His ambassadors to be consistent in their Christian living. It is one thing to be an ambassador from the United States to a friendly nation like England. It is quite another matter to be an ambassador in a hot spot like the Sudan. The same is true for those of us who are Christ's ambassadors in difficult places today. It takes a special person to be His ambassador in a combat zone. That assignment demands not only pure character and proper conduct but personal actions that are consistent with those of Christ's.

AN AMBASSADOR'S COMMUNICATION

Effective ambassadors have mastered the art of communication. They are in constant, daily communication with the State Department. At the same time, they constantly communicate with leaders of the nation to which they are assigned. In most situations, ambassadors are bilingual, speaking both the language of home and the native language of the country where they are serving.

Now, if we are to be effective ambassadors for Christ, we ourselves must be in constant, daily contact with headquarters. We must also be communicating the wishes, desires, and commands of our Leader to those among whom we live. Otherwise, we have fallen short of our calling and our task.

AN AMBASSADOR'S CONSIDERATION

Ambassadors are considered and chosen on the basis of their ability to be men and women of diplomacy. The art of diplomacy is high on the list of their most important objectives. They are most effective when they are winsome as they go about their work. We certainly would not want someone representing our nation who was abrasive and constantly agitating others.

How much more should we, as Christ's ambassadors, be winsome as we go about our own work and witness. We should be the most appealing and welcoming people found anywhere. In fact, the Bible says we are to be "the fragrance of Christ" to those around us (2 Corinthians 2:15).

As Christ's ambassadors, we have a single purpose: to "implore [others] on Christ's behalf; [to] be reconciled to God" (NIV). This is our assignment. This is our task. In order to accomplish it, we must take on all the characteristics of an ambassador. We have been appointed by our King to be His ambassadors. Let's make sure we live up to our calling.

As you memorize this verse, meditate on all the qualities of an ambassador and, as you go about your own work and witness this week, represent Him in a manner worthy of your calling.

43 INTEGRITY: DON'T LEAVE HOME WITHOUT IT!

He who walks with integrity walks securely,
but he who perverts his ways will become known.

PROVERBS 10:9

*W*hat is the single most important trait of a person who desires to truly make a difference in our world today? Some would say it is intellect. After all, knowledge is power in many ways. Others contend it is intensity, that spirit of conquest accompanied by a passion that becomes contagious. Still others suggest it is insight, good old common sense, along with the ability to clearly see certain issues. However, I contend the most important trait is integrity. We have all known people along life's journey who have incredible intellect, but no integrity, and they are no longer in the race. Others possessing amazing intensity and passion but little integrity have gone the same way. The same is true of people with keen insight but no integrity. Integrity is our most valuable commodity.

Integrity is that state or quality of being complete, and

it is freedom from corrupting influences or motives. The thesaurus equates it with such words as *honesty*, *completeness*, and *incorruptibility*. Yes, "he who walks with integrity walks securely."

Each of us lives in four distinct spheres of life and influence. You live in a *private* world. There is a part of you where no one really goes. Not even those closest to us—our husbands, our wives—know all our private thoughts. No one invades your private world except you . . . and the God who knows all your private thoughts. You also live in a *personal* world. This is the part of you that you share with a small circle of immediate family and perhaps a few friends who really know you intimately. Next comes your *professional* world. This existence consists of dozens or even scores of men and women who, although they do not know you personally, much less privately, know you in a professional setting. Finally, you live in a *public* world. This is the world in which people have never met you personally or dealt with you professionally, but they have formed an opinion about you. We call this our public persona. The reality of these four spheres raises an important question: where is integrity in life rooted?

INTEGRITY IS ROOTED IN ONE'S PRIVATE LIFE

Integrity stems from an inner code, not an outer promotion. Integrity is rooted in that private life we develop alone with God in the secret, hidden place. We often hear architects, engineers, or builders say, "This building has structural integrity." That is, the public beauty of a tall skyscraper relies on its private, unseen foundation that is dug deep into the earth and solidly constructed. It is that hidden life of a building that brings structural integrity. It is the hidden life of an orange tree, that unseen root system that digs deep into the earth, that produces those juicy, delectable fruits. And so it is with us. Integrity is rooted in the private life.

What made a man like Billy Graham so influential and so trusted for so many decades? Was it his intellect? Was it his intensity? No. It was, without question, his unblemished integrity that earned him a prolonged hearing. King Solomon had it right: "The integrity of the upright will guide them" (Proverbs 11:3).

INTEGRITY IS REFLECTED IN ONE'S PERSONAL LIFE

Once integrity is rooted in our private life, it begins to be reflected in our relationships with those closest to us. Many seem to think that integrity is rooted in these close interpersonal experiences, but it is not. It is only reflected there, if, in fact, we are men and women of integrity. If you want to know whether I have integrity, ask my wife or my daughters who really know me in the intimacy of close family relationships. Integrity does not find its roots in the personal world. However, it is certainly reflected there.

INTEGRITY IS REINFORCED IN ONE'S PROFESSIONAL LIFE

What about your professional life, that sphere of life that is ever widening? If you have a hidden life where your own integrity finds its roots, it will not only be reflected in your close relationships with those around you, but it will also be reinforced in your day-to-day dealings in the work world. Integrity is reinforced on the anvil of personal experience and practiced in the marketplace.

Our greatest opportunity to make a difference and engage our culture is out in the marketplace. It is imperative that, as Christians, we are men and women of integrity in the professional world around us. There is a small and decreasing percentage of people in our cities in church on Sunday mornings. However, on Monday, multitudes enter the marketplace. They take note of individuals of integrity. Integrity is not rooted in our professional life; it is only reinforced there. That is, if we truly possess it.

INTEGRITY IS REVEALED IN ONE'S PUBLIC LIFE

Once we are thrust into the public arena, it is too late to look for integrity. If we do not already possess it, it is too late. However, some seek to put a spin on their personal promotion in a hopeless effort to somehow lead others to believe they are people of integrity. But integrity is not rooted in spin, it's rooted in our private world. Solomon's words ring true today: "He who walks with integrity walks securely, but he who perverts his ways will become known."

When integrity is rooted in the private world, it is reflected in the personal world, reinforced in the professional world, and, ultimately, revealed in the public world for the glory of the God whom we love and serve.

As you memorize this verse, meditate on your own private life. Bring focus to that time alone with God, to your hidden life. Then "all these things shall be added to you" (Matthew 6:33).

44   THE WORD BECAME FLESH

And the Word became flesh and dwelt among us,
and we beheld His glory, the glory as of the only
begotten of the Father, full of grace and truth.

JOHN 1:14

*W*ho is this "Word" spoken of in the opening verses of John's gospel? Was it another one of the prophets sent from God to deliver His message to us? Was it some high and holy angel who had been dwelling in the celestials for millennia? No, this Word is infinitely more than any created being. This is God Himself, stepping out of heaven, clothing Himself in human flesh, and entering human history. John is explicit about His identity: "In the beginning was the Word, and the Word was with God, and the Word was God" (John 1:1).

Other passages in Scripture expand on this truth about Jesus, the God-man. Probing the depths of this truth, Paul said that God "has highly exalted Him and given Him the name which is above every name, that . . . every knee should bow . . . and that every tongue should confess that Jesus Christ is Lord, to the glory of God the Father" (Philippians

2:9–11). To the Colossians, Paul said that Christ "is the image of the invisible God . . . For by Him all things were created . . . and in Him all things consist . . . that in all things He may have the preeminence" (1:15–18). And the writer of Hebrews relates that He "purged our sins [and] sat down at the right hand of the Majesty on high" (1:3).

The incarnation, that period of thirty-three years when God invaded earth clothed in flesh and bone, is one of the most condescending displays of divine love to be found anywhere at any time. In the incarnation, we marvel at God's garment, grace, and glory.

GOD'S GARMENT

"The Word became flesh." Jesus came down to where we are so we could go to where He is! He came to us and took on our flesh. He was not God *and* man as He walked the ways of this world. He was the unique God-man. As God, He walked on water, calmed the storm, healed the sick, and rose from the dead. As man, He got thirsty and tired; He felt sorrow and pain.

Think about it. Jesus came, not clinging to all the brightness of His glory, not shunning us for our sinful condition, but humbling Himself to become a servant and to clothe Himself in flesh. By doing so, He would be able to say, "I understand" every emotion, temptation, and pain we experience.

After all, if God were to become a man, we would certainly expect Him to have an unusual and unique entrance into our existence. He came, not as a full-grown man, but as a helpless, tiny seed planted in the womb of a young Jewish virgin. Jesus was born not in a clean and sterile environment on starched white sheets, but in the dung and filth of a Bethlehem stable where sickness, disease, and even death were all possibilities. This is amazing condescension: in Jesus, God Himself took on the garment of human flesh.

GOD'S GRACE

In the incarnation, we also see God's amazing grace. Yes, He "dwelt among us . . . full of grace and truth." The word translated *dwelt* means "to take up temporary residence as though one lived in a tent." This was our Lord's mission. He came here, for a time, in order to pay the penalty for our sin, that He might bring us to the Father. Thus, He "dwelt among us," but only temporarily in human flesh.

The text continues to inform us that Jesus was "full of grace." *Grace* is defined as "unmerited favor." Jesus was full of grace. There is a difference between mercy and grace. *Mercy* is not getting what we do deserve. *Grace* is getting what we do not deserve. Jesus' love is always manifested in His grace. Consistently in Scripture we find Him extending this undeserved and unmerited favor upon sinners. Even at the cross we find Him praying for the forgiveness of those who were persecuting and killing Him. The Word, who became flesh, truly was "full of grace."

Our Lord was also "full of . . . truth." In fact, He was the embodiment of truth. It is only when His grace leads us to know the truth that we are truly free. Jesus came, not to talk to us about God, but to show us what God was like so that the simplest mind might know the Father as intimately as the most intelligent academic.

GOD'S GLORY

In Christ's incarnation, we also catch a glimpse of His glory: "We beheld His glory, the glory as of the only begotten of the Father." There is little doubt that John, now an old man, was reminiscing about the Transfiguration when he penned these words. He had been there, along with his brother James and Simon Peter, when our Lord was transfigured into His glorified body. John saw "His glory" all right! On that mountain John witnessed Jesus as "His face shone like the sun, and His clothes became as white as the light" (Matthew 17:2).

The incarnation of Christ should not be thought of as a past, historical phenomenon. In a sense, it can be a continuing experience. This same Jesus who was born in Bethlehem, who took on human flesh, longs to be born again in our hearts. His desire is to take up residency in you, to dwell in your heart today. Paul reveled in this thought when he said, "Christ in you, the hope of glory" (Colossians 1:27). Have you personally "beheld His glory" in yourself?

As you memorize this verse, meditate on Christ's amazing condescension. He laid aside His glory to enter human flesh . . . for me . . . for *you*. 🖎

45 THE BIG TEN

*"I am the LORD your God, who brought you out
of the land of Egypt, out of the house of bondage.
You shall have no other gods before Me."*

EXODUS 20:2–3

There are several hundred commandments in the Torah, but the Big Ten are found here in Exodus 20. We are observing an intentional and intensive assault on the Ten Commandments in our Western culture today. Any reference to them is being systematically removed from our public squares, our public school classrooms, and almost every other place imaginable. However, a trip to our nation's capital finds these Ten Commandments etched in granite on government buildings, carved in mahogany in public libraries, and even center stage on the wall above where the Supreme Court justices hold court each day. These public displays are living testimonies to our Founding Fathers' faith and to the principles that made this the greatest nation on earth. The Ten Commandments have, through the years of our republic, been the thread with which the fabric of our great nation has been woven. The Ten Commandments have served as the building blocks of most every civil and decent society for more than three thousand years.

We all understand the importance of rules and standards in our daily lives. Can you imagine a football game without sideline boundary markers? What kind of order would there be in a game where the running back could leave the playing field, run up the stadium steps, go out through the parking lot, enter the field from another angle, and score a touchdown? Boundaries are a part of our everyday life. Homebuilders have building codes or boundaries, to which they must adhere. We all need absolutes. Civilized society needs boundaries in which to exist. When does a train move most freely? A train is most free when it stays on the tracks that have been set out for it, not when it is trying to move through a field. The same is true with us. Like the train on its tracks, we move most freely when we have clearly defined tracks or standards by which to live.

Our memory verse in this chapter includes the first commandment. Why? Why not the third . . . or the seventh . . . or the tenth? Because if we get the first commandment right, all the others have a way of falling into place. This is true for the first four, those that define our relationship with God, that is, the vertical ones. Getting the first commandment right also helps our relationships with others, which are addressed in the horizontal commandments, or the last six. When we give the Lord priority in our lives, we will not have difficulty with stealing or lying or adultery or any of the others. The command to love God is listed first for a very significant reason: this first commandment of the Big Ten offers four very important principles for living the Christian life.

PRINCIPLE #1: GOD IS PRESENT

The presentation of the Ten Commandments begins with an amazing declaration: "I AM." When Moses was called by God from the burning bush to be the great emancipator of God's people, Moses asked, "When I get back to the Israelites, who shall I say has sent me? What is your name?" God replied, "Tell him I AM has sent you" (Exodus 3:13–14). God is ever present, from eternity past to eternity future. For a brief thirty-three-year span in history, He stepped out of space into our physical realm. But He has always been and always will be the great I AM.

By the time the Israelites' journey brought them to Exodus 20, they had almost forgotten their heritage. It was there and then that the ever-present God delivered to them His Ten Commandments; He wrote them on a tablet with His own finger. God is still present today. He is not someone who simply appeared one time in history and is nowhere today. He is still the great I AM.

PRINCIPLE #2: GOD IS PERSONAL

He is "the Lord *your* God." This word is singular in Hebrew, indicating that God desires a one-on-one relationship with you. Many believe the Christian life is about religion. Others think it is about ritual; that is, the performance of certain outer, perfunctory duties. But the Christian life is really about a relationship—a vital, living, and personal relationship with the Lord Jesus Christ.

The purpose of the law was never to save us. It is erroneous to believe that any of us can keep all God's commandments. In fact, the Scripture teaches that, if we break just one of them, we are guilty of breaking all of them (James 2:10). Paul, in the New Testament, said the law was simply "our tutor to bring us to Christ, that we might be justified by faith" (Galatians 3:24). The law is there to teach us how we all fall short of meeting God's standards, and how much we need a Savior. We could never save ourselves by keeping the law.

God said, "I am the Lord your God." But is He? Do you know Him with the intimacy of Father and child? Do you know Him, who is life and life eternal? The only way we can abide by the commandments and make them a matter of the heart is to know Him in a personal relationship. He is not just always present, but He is also personal.

PRINCIPLE #3: GOD IS POWERFUL

The Almighty God reminded Moses that He was the one who "brought you out of the land of Egypt, out of the house of bondage." He was the One who sent the plagues upon Egypt. He was the One pictured in the deliverance provided by the Passover Lamb. He was the One who parted the Red Sea. He was the One who led the people of Israel with a cloud by day and a pillar of fire by night. He was the One who fed them daily with manna. He was the One who brought water from the rock. How prone we all are to forget how powerful our God is and all He has done for us in the past.

President Woodrow Wilson once said, "A nation which does not remember what it was yesterday does not know what it is today nor what it is trying to do. We are trying to do a futile thing if we do not know where we came from or what we have been about." Here in this first commandment God is encouraging us to remember what awesome things He has done for us in the past. When we do, we can have power in the present and confidence in the future.

PRINCIPLE #4: GOD IS PREEMINENT

"You shall have no other gods before Me." God could not be more specific. He demands preeminence. Allowing Him to rule on the throne of our hearts is to be the priority of every believer's life. When this happens, when we love the Lord with all our heart, soul, and mind, we are amazed at how "all these [other] things" are added to us (Matthew 22:37; Matthew 6:33).

The ancient Hebrews, however, had a tendency of falling into polytheism, or into worshiping other gods. Old gods never seem to die. They simply continue to repackage themselves and show up in succeeding generations. A "god" is anyone or anything that enjoys your primary devotion. Some make a god of their possessions; there is nothing wrong with possessing things unless they begin to possess you. Others find their god in promiscuity; sex has become the god many worship in our modern world. Politics is the god of some. Others bow at the altar of pleasure in our sports-mad and entertainment-crazed world. But God warns, "You shall have no other gods before Me." He must have priority over everything in our lives.

Once someone approached Jesus of Nazareth and asked Him to identify the greatest of all God's commandments. In a single statement, the Ten Commandments, not to mention all of the 613 commandments in the Torah, were reduced down to two. Jesus said, "'You shall love the LORD your God with all your heart, with all your soul, and with all your mind.' This is the first and great commandment. And the second is like it: 'You shall love your neighbor as yourself.' On these two commandments hang all the Law and the Prophets" (Matthew 22:37–40). There you have it; the vertical relationship we have with God (Exodus 20:1–11) and the horizontal relationships we have with each other (Exodus 20:12–17) addressed in the Great Commandment.

Let's put Christ first in our lives so that we do not join the company of those who seem to forget, in time, that we enjoy blessings with our heavenly Father because Christ died to win them. When Christ came, He took these commandments and made them a matter of the heart. Love is the theme, the eternal theme.

As you memorize this verse, meditate on each of the Ten Commandments one by one. And remember that "the greatest of these is love" (1 Corinthians 13:13).

46 THE MODEL PRAYER

"In this manner, therefore, pray:
Our Father in heaven, hallowed be Your name."

MATTHEW 6:9

According to the Bible, the disciples asked our Lord to teach them to do only one thing. After living with Him for three years, traveling over all Galilee and Judea, and eating hundreds of meals together, they only asked to be taught one thing. They never asked Jesus to teach them to preach. They did not ask Him to teach them to evangelize or to heal the sick. The only thing they ever asked Jesus to teach them is recorded for us in Luke 11:1. They requested, "Lord, teach us to pray." The disciples were smart enough to know that this was the secret of His life. They had seen Him on many occasions slip away from them into the mountains to pray. They had observed Him on occasion praying all through the night. They saw Him pray before every great undertaking and after every great accomplishment. They knew that if they could master prayer, they would then know how to preach, how to evangelize, and how to do any of the other necessary tasks of carrying out their mission and calling in life.

Perhaps there is no other prayer that has been recited by as many people, at as many times, in as many places, as this prayer—commonly called "The Lord's Prayer." However, it is often referred to as the "Model Prayer." The Lord's Prayer is found in John 17, where we have the record of His high intercessory prayer for us on the eve of the Crucifixion. This prayer, found in Matthew 6:9–13, is a model and guide for our own prayer life. It contains a prayer for God's glory and a prayer for our good.

A PRAYER FOR GOD'S GLORY

This prayer begins with the element of *worship*: "hallowed be Your name" (Matthew 6:9). The word *hallowed* means "sanctified; that which is set apart." The name of the Lord is unlike any other name. It is holy. Jesus taught us here that prayer is to be entered into with a reverent and worshipful attitude as though we are coming to a King.

The prayer also includes the element of *witness*: "Your kingdom come" (v. 10). There is a kingdom of grace and a coming kingdom of glory presented to us in the Bible. When we pray this prayer, we are praying for those around us who have never entered God's kingdom of grace by being born again. We are also joining those saints of all the ages who have looked for our "blessed hope" and His glorious appearing" (Titus 2:13). Jesus is coming again to set up His glorious kingdom. Thus, we join John, as he prayed from Patmos: "Even so, come, Lord Jesus" (Revelation 22:20).

This model prayer for God's glory also entails the element of the *will*: "Your will be done" (v. 10). In a previous chapter we heard our Lord praying beneath those ancient olive trees of Gethsemane's garden, "not My will, but Yours, be done" (Luke 22:42). Jesus taught us here that we cannot come to God in prayer with a selfish spirit, bent only on our way and our will. We must come to Him humbly in a spirit of submission, joining Jesus in praying, "Your will be done."

A PRAYER FOR OUR GOOD

The remainder of this model prayer consists of our personal petitions that result not only in God's glory, but in our own good. We ask for *provision*: "Give us this day our daily bread" (v. 11). We are dependent upon our heavenly Father to meet our basic needs of life. We cannot approach Him with an independent spirit of self-sufficiency. It is also important to note it is "daily" bread at issue here. One of the reasons many believers fall by the wayside is that they forget this point. The manna fell daily in the wilderness and was only edible on that day. What we take in today of the Bible, the Bread of Life, sustains us for today. As we ask God for provisions, remember He supplies "daily bread."

There is also a petition here for *pardon*: "forgive us our debts, as we forgive our debtors" (v. 12). Thus, we come to God in prayer with a penitent spirit and not just a dependent one. We cannot come to Him with unconfessed and unforgiven sin in our lives. Once again note that every word of this prayer is there for a reason. We are asking God to forgive us "as we forgive our debtors." But do we really mean this? We need to think deeply about what we are praying here. Some are prone to say, "Well, I will forgive her, but I won't have anything else to do with her." Is that really the way we wish for God to forgive us? Think about this the next time you pray this model prayer.

We also find a petition here for *protection*: "And do not lead us into temptation, but deliver us from the evil one" (v. 13). We need God to lead us. He will never lead us to do wrong. There is a difference between the temptations of life and the trials of life that come our way. Trials often come from God to teach us to stand; temptation comes from the devil to cause us to stumble. We need God's leadership and deliverance in our daily lives.

We begin this prayer by saying, "Our Father" (v. 9). The foundation of all true prayers is in these first two words of the model prayer. If you cannot say "Our Father," you will never have an effective prayer life. And you cannot say "Our Father" unless you have been born into His family by trusting in His Son for the forgiveness of your sin and the gift of eternal life with Him.

"Our Father." Yes, we are not beggars cowering down at a back door looking for a handout from some cosmic benefactor. We are God's children, seated at His table, making our requests known to Him (Philippians 4:6). No wonder we are invited to come with boldness to His throne of grace (Hebrews 4:16). Prayer has a twofold purpose: it is for God's glory and our good.

As you memorize this verse, meditate on the fact that this is but a pattern for our praying. Jesus never actually told us to pray this prayer. He said, "in this manner, pray ..." (Matthew 6:5). It is but a model for us to follow as we join the apostles in asking, "Lord, teach us to pray."

47 A NEW SONG OF REDEMPTION

And they sang a new song saying:
"You are worthy to take the scroll,
And to open its seals;
For You were slain,
And have redeemed us to God by Your blood
Out of every tribe and tongue and people and nation."

REVELATION 5:9

⬦⬦⬦⬦⬦⬦⬦⬦⬦⬦⬦⬦⬦⬦

*O*ur limited minds can scarcely grasp the thought that Christ redeemed us with the purchase price of His own blood. The writer of Hebrews reminded us that it is "not with the blood of goats and calves, but with His own blood He entered the most Holy Place once for all, having obtained eternal redemption" (9:12). Simon Peter elaborated on the point, saying, "You were not redeemed with corruptible things, like silver or gold, from your aimless conduct received by tradition from your fathers, but with the precious blood of Christ, as of a lamb without blemish and without spot" (1 Peter 1:18–19).

It is no wonder we will be singing this "new song" in heaven. Jesus alone is worthy to be the object of our worship. He is the only One who was slain and who redeemed us by His own blood. This verse reveals to us the hope of redemption as well as the scope of redemption.

THE HOPE OF REDEMPTION

Our hope of being redeemed is found in Christ and in Christ alone. As Paul said, "In Him we have redemption through His blood, the forgiveness of sins, according to the riches of His grace" (Ephesians 1:7).

Redemption is the scarlet thread that is woven throughout the entire Bible. The word *redemption* comes from *agora*, the Greek word for "the marketplace." In its verb form in Revelation 5:9, the word indicates that Jesus Christ entered the marketplace and purchased us out of the market to be His very own. How much do you think you are worth to Him? What would He pay for you? Our redemption had a large price tag affixed. The cost was Christ's own blood.

In this fifth chapter of Revelation, we come upon one of the great worship experiences of all time. What is it that gives us access to Christ's presence in worship? Is it the observance of certain religious rituals, the adoration of certain images or icons? The Bible is explicit: it is the blood of the Lord Jesus that gives us access to His throne of worship, not only in the unfolding scene in Revelation, but also in our own private devotional time. Our only hope of redemption is in Christ and His shed blood.

THE SCOPE OF REDEMPTION

Who is covered by this purchase price? Is it only for those on one end of the economic or social spectrum? Is it only for those who look like we look and act like we act? The new song of heaven declares that the scope of God's redemption extends to "every tribe and tongue and people and nation." Jesus reaches out to those in the most remote tribal regions of our world. His redemption knows no language barrier. It is for every tongue. And, yes, it is for every people and every nation.

I remember vividly the first time I ever saw this word *redemption*. I was about eight years of age, and I desperately wanted a new baseball glove. This was in the day before we used credit cards to the extent they are used today. Most of us use those plastic cards in order to earn points so that we can acquire certain goods or services without actually having to pay cash for them. Back in the "olden days," we had what was called "S&H Green Stamps." They served the same purpose. One day while browsing through my mother's catalog, I saw a genuine leather baseball glove that could be mine with two and a half books of Green Stamps. Thus, I persuaded my mom to let me have the Green Stamps she received from grocery shopping, gasoline servicing, and the like. Finally, after a few months, I had licked and stuck enough Green Stamps into my books to acquire my glove.

One Saturday, my dad drove me to the southside of

Fort Worth. We pulled into a parking lot adjacent to a large, white concrete block building. As we were walking into the building, I noted over the door the words "S&H Green Stamp Redemption Center." I had never seen that word *redemption* before and had no idea what it meant. Upon entering the building, I approached the counter and laid out my two and a half books of Green Stamps along with the page of the catalog with the picture of the baseball glove. The lady began thumbing through each page. My heart started fluttering. What if I had skipped a page? Next, she disappeared into a back room. Minutes later she returned with a square box. She shoved it across the counter in my direction. I opened it and, sure enough, there was a genuine leather baseball glove inside.

I put it on my hand and started patting the pocket with my other fist. I did this all the way home. A teenager up the street had told me that I should put some linseed oil in the pocket, wrap a ball inside, and tie it off with a large rubber band at night to form the pocket. I think I actually slept with that glove the first several nights I had it. I redeemed that glove with two and a half books of S&H Green Stamps.

And so our dear Lord one day stepped up to redemption's counter . . . for you. His Father sent Him. So down He came, past solar systems and constellations and through measureless space. Down still farther to become a helpless seed planted in the womb of a young virgin to grow for nine months. Down yet farther, to be born in the dung and filth of a Bethlehem stable. Then down even farther, to go about doing good, only to be beaten and mocked, spit upon and scorned, and to finally walk up to redemption's counter. There He put down His own blood to redeem you. Why? So He could take you home with Him!

This is the message of the gospel. This is why we will one day join that celestial choir in singing a new song, "You are worthy . . . for You were slain and have redeemed us to God by Your blood out of every tribe and tongue and people and nation."

As you memorize this verse, meditate on the tremendous price our Lord paid to purchase you out of the marketplace and take you home with Him.

48   GOD CALLING!

And the Spirit and the bride say, "'Come!" And let him
who hears say, "Come!" And let him who thirsts come.
Whoever desires, let him take the water of life freely.

REVELATION 22:17

*T*he Spirit of God and the bride of Christ both beckon us to come to the Lord Jesus. The bride is clearly a reference to the church in the New Testament, that body of born-again believers who one day will be reunited with their Bridegroom, the Lord Jesus Christ. It is the supreme task of the church to call people to come to Christ. It is also the Spirit who says, "Come." While the church issues this outward call, the Spirit of the Living God issues the inward call to hearts. They work in tandem: "the Spirit and the bride, say 'Come!'"

In the eighth chapter of Romans, we are introduced to a chain reaction effect. Those God foreknew, He predestined. Those He predestined, He called. Those He called, He justified. And those He justified, He also glorified. This mysterious calling of God upon our hearts is a significant part of His total redemptive plan. It is not as though we are somehow neutral in all of this and God chooses some to go to heaven and certain others to go to hell. That is a false assumption because Scripture clearly teaches that none of us are neutral. We are not suspended in some sort of limbo. In fact, we have all gone our own way (Isaiah 53:6). We have all sinned and come short of God's glory (Romans 3:23). Our salvation is wholly of grace through faith in Christ alone (Ephesians 2:8).

Thus, we have two distinct yet related callings: the Spirit is saying, "Come," and the church, the bride, is echoing the same call as well.

THE INWARD CALL

The Bible says that the Spirit is calling us to come to Christ. This is the inward call to our hearts. I could beg you on my knees, with tears in my eyes, describing the horrors of hell and the wonders of heaven, but you will not truly come to Christ unless the Spirit is drawing you. It was our Lord Himself who said, "No one can come to Me unless the Father who sent Me draws him" (John 6:44). Do you recall what the Lord said to Peter immediately after he made his great confession at Caesarea Philippi? Jesus pronounced a blessing on him and then said, "Flesh and blood has not revealed this to you, but My Father who is in heaven" (Matthew 16:17). Later Paul would add, "For as many as are led by the Spirit of God, these are sons of God" (Romans 8:14). And to the Galatians, Paul said that it "pleased God, who separated me from my mother's womb, and called me through His grace" (Galatians 1:15). Not to be left out, Peter weighed in, saying, "You are a chosen generation, a royal priesthood, a holy nation, His own special people, that you may proclaim the praises of Him who called you out of darkness into His marvelous light" (1 Peter 2:9). Later, in this same letter, Peter said that the God of all grace had "called us to His eternal glory" (5:10).

One of the most beautiful illustrations of the Spirit's calling people to Christ is found in Acts 16. Here we are introduced to a very successful businesswoman named Lydia. Paul was preaching and issuing the outward call, and the Bible reveals that Lydia, whose "heart the Lord opened" (Acts 16:14 KJV), embraced the gospel message. Yes, the Spirit speaks to our hearts with His inward call, saying, "Come!"

THE OUTWARD CALL

Here is a wonderful partnership of the Spirit of God working in and through the church of the Lord Jesus Christ. God has chosen to use the church to issue the outward call to the hearts of men and women across the world. Not only does the Spirit call us to come to Christ, but the bride says, "Come!" as well.

This is actually what happened at the grave of Lazarus, one of our Lord's closest earthly friends. Many nights the

Lord had stayed in his home in Bethany. Many meals He had shared at his table along with his sisters, Mary and Martha. Now Lazarus was dead and buried. Jesus came upon the scene and found the funeral party in deep mourning. There was the outward call; there was something for the people there to do. They were to roll away the large stone that sealed the tomb, but only Jesus could bring Lazarus back to life. Thus, after the stone was rolled away, Jesus issued the inward call. Jesus spoke to Lazarus, saying, "Lazarus, come forth" (John 11:43). And he did! The church's responsibility in the outward call is to roll away the stones today. As we call people to faith, we seek to roll away stones of indifference, stones of unbelief, stones of presumption, stones of pride, and stones of procrastination. Our apologetics and our witness enable men and women to be more sensitive to hearing Christ's inward call to their hearts.

My mentor and pastoral predecessor W. A. Criswell approached this complicated issue with a rather simple understanding. I often heard him say that those high and lofty theological words like *election*, *predestination*, and *sanctification* were "up there." They belonged to God. We were to leave them there and not speculate upon them. Words such as *grace*, *faith*, *repentance*, and the like were "down here." These are the words with which we should deal. The older I have become, the more I think he was right in his assessment. Our part is to believe and receive.

For the Bible says, "As many as received Him, to them He gave the right to become children of God, to those who believe in His name" (John 1:12).

As you memorize this verse, meditate on the fact that the Spirit is calling. Listen to what the prophet Elijah referred to as that "still small voice" (1 Kings 19:12 KJV). It is not audible. However, when you hear it, it is unmistakable. God is calling.

49   HERE COMES THE JUDGE!

For we must all appear before the judgment seat of Christ,
that each one may receive the things done in the body,
according to what he has done, whether good or bad.

2 CORINTHIANS 5:10

*P*erhaps there is no other subject more relegated to the back recesses of our minds than the fact that each of us will one day stand before the supreme Judge of all the earth. In His court there are no mistrials, no appeals, no probations, no adjudicated sentences, and no hung juries. It is the one court where ultimate and perfect justice will prevail.

The subject of this final judgment is also one of the most confusing ones in all Scripture. However, when we understand that there are at least four coming judgments delineated in the Bible, it brings more focus and greater understanding of what lies ahead. Here comes the Judge.

THE JUDGMENT OF SIN

The first judgment related to us has already taken place. It is the judgment of the believer's sin. Jesus said, "Most assuredly, I say to you, he who hears My word and believes in Him who sent Me has everlasting life, and shall not come into judgment, but has passed from death into life" (John 5:24). Our sins were judged in Christ as He hung on Calvary's cross. He suffered for our sins. He paid our penalty. He took our place and bore the wrath of God's judgment of sin in His own body on the cross. As Paul indicated, "[God] made Him who knew no sin to become sin for us" (2 Corinthians 5:21).

God judged the believer's sin one dark day outside the city walls of Jerusalem when Christ died our death so that we could eternally live His life. It is no wonder the great apostle Paul began the informative eighth chapter of Romans by saying, "There is therefore now no condemnation [no judgment] to those who are in Christ Jesus" (v.1). No condemnation! I want to shout my thanks to God for those two words and the truth that is so undeserved and unmerited. Christ died in my place and took the punishment and judgment of my sins in His own body.

THE JUDGMENT OF SAINTS

The fact that Jesus stood in our place at the judgment of sin does not mean we will not stand before Him, the righteous Judge, at the judgment of the saints. This is referred to as the judgment seat of Christ. Paul speaks of this in 2 Corinthians: "We must all appear before the judgment seat of Christ, that each one may receive the things done in the body, whether good or bad" (5:10).

At this judgment, taking place immediately after Christ's return, our works will be judged, not our sins. Our sins were judged at the cross. Our eternal salvation is not at issue at this judgment. Here, we believers will each give an account of ourselves before God, and the degree of our rewards will be assessed and determined by the One who judges all things well. One of the most beautiful aspects about this judgment is that "we have an Advocate with the Father, Jesus Christ the righteous" (1 John 2:1).

Christ—our Advocate, our own personal defense attorney—will plead our case before the judgment bar. The good news is that God cannot and will not see our sins because of the blood of Jesus.

THE JUDGMENT OF STATES

The judgment of the states, better known as the judgment of nations, takes place at the conclusion of the period of the Great Tribulation. It is this judgment the prophet Joel alluded to when he said that God will "judge all the surrounding nations" (Joel 3:12). This judgment determines who will enter the millennial reign of Christ. At issue here is the treatment of Israel during the period of tribulation. Jesus said, "Inasmuch as you did it to one of the least of these My brethren, you did it to Me" (Matthew 25:40).

The Bible says that Israel is still "the apple of [God's] eye" (Zechariah 2:8). In fact, God says of Israel and His chosen people that "My eyes and My heart will be there perpetually" (2 Chronicles 7:16). Those who are saved in this judgment are the sheep that "inherit the kingdom prepared for [them]" (Matthew 25:34). The lost, the goats, are those who "will go away into everlasting punishment" (v. 46). Those entering the coming millennial kingdom of Christ will consist only of the saved.

THE JUDGMENT OF SINNERS

The apostle John was the only one of his peers who did not meet a martyr's death. At over ninety years of age, he was exiled to the lonely island of Patmos by the Romans where God opened heaven to him and showed him what was to come. John put it thus: "I saw a great white throne and Him who sat on it, from whose face the earth and the heaven fled away. And there was found no place for them. And I saw the dead, small and great, standing before God, and the books were opened. . . . And anyone not found written in the Book of Life was cast into the lake of fire" (Revelation 20:11–12, 15). This great white throne judgment follows the thousand-year reign of Christ's kingdom. Only those who have not placed their trust in Christ alone for their salvation will stand before this judgment bar.

Every lost person who has ever lived will stand before

Christ to give account for their lives. The Lamb's Book of Life will be opened. This book contains the names of all those who come to know Christ as Lord and Savior during their earthly pilgrimage. The lost who stand before God will see that there was room where their names could have been listed.

Think of the billions of people who will stand before the great white throne. How long will it take for them to come, one at a time, before God and give account for everything they have ever done? It will not matter. Time will be no more. Eternity will have begun. These lost souls will be pronounced guilty, the degree of their punishment will be determined, and they will be cast into a godless eternity of darkness forever. Lost beyond hope, lost beyond help, lost beyond time, lost beyond Christ . . . lost. Forever lost.

Here comes the Judge. Christ is coming to judge the world. Only Christ is the righteous Judge. None of us can stand in judgment of anyone else's heart. Ultimately, we can rest in the truth of Genesis 18:25: "Shall not the Judge of all the earth do right?"

When all is said and done, the only question that really matters in this world—and the next—is this one: Is your name in the Book?

As you memorize this verse, meditate on the wonderful privilege that we, as believers, have in Christ, our Advocate. And ask yourself the question: Is my name in the Book?

50   HEAVEN

For our citizenship is in heaven, from which
we also eagerly wait for the Savior, the Lord Jesus Christ.

PHILIPPIANS 3:20

❖❖❖❖❖❖❖❖❖❖❖❖❖❖❖❖❖

*W*e live in a world where an increasing number of people do not believe in an eternal hell, a place of everlasting punishment. A frequently asked question is "How could a loving God allow anyone to go to hell?" My problem has always been just the opposite. By that I mean, I have no problem believing in hell. But how could there be such a wonderful place like heaven? How could the love and grace of God be so awesome as to make it possible for a sinner like me to spend eternity in such a place?

John saw "a door standing open in heaven" (Revelation 4:1) from his lonely rock island of exile called Patmos. God has left us a few open doors in Scripture though which we can catch a glimpse of what awaits us there. Let's take a look into what lies ahead for those who trust in Him.

HEAVEN IS A PLACE OF REALITY

Heaven is real. Throughout time God has implanted within the soul of man a longing for such a place. All primitive people believed in an afterlife. In ages gone by, the ancient cave dwellers depicted such in paintings on the walls of their caves. More than three thousand years ago the Egyptians buried their pharaohs with supplies, eating utensils, weapons, and even servants in their quest for a life that is beyond this one. The American Indians had their "happy hunting grounds" where they believed the departed lived again. God has implanted and instilled within the very being of man a desire for more from life than what we have on earth.

This longing continues today. Every time a scientist enters the laboratory with a strong motivation driving them to find a cure for cancer or AIDS, it is an expression of a subconscious hunger for a world that is free of pain and disease. Heaven is such a place. Every social worker sincerely motivated to abolish rancid living conditions has a subconscious longing for a world without poverty and homelessness. Every environmentalist moved to clean and purify the environment is on a quest for a world that is pure and beautiful. Statesmen who sit around peace tables in the hot spots of our world are simply in search of a world without war and conflict.

The human soul needs heaven, and it alone can finish what we leave unfinished here. Sir Isaac Newton—whose mind, it has been said, could master the most profound truths as easily as most of us can master our ABCs—once said, "I seem to be only a boy picking up a few small pebbles along the shore while the vast ocean of truth lies unexplored before me."

Heaven is real. It is a place. Jesus said, "I go to prepare a place for you" (John 14:2). It is a real, tangible place.

HEAVEN IS A PLACE OF RADIANCE

Heaven is not simply a place. It is a prepared place (John 14:2), and it is beautiful. God loves beauty or He would never have made things on this sin-cursed earth so beautiful. John got a glimpse of heaven's beauty one day and wrote down a few simple symbols that our poor finite minds could understand: "Its wall was of jasper; and the city was pure gold, like clear glass" (Revelation 21:18). It is no wonder that earlier the apostle Paul had said, "Eye has not seen, nor ear heard, nor have entered into the heart of man the things which God has prepared for those who love Him" (1 Corinthians 2:9). Could it be that heaven is "like clear glass" because there will be nothing to hide there?

Heaven is a place of unparalleled beauty and radiance. The book of Revelation is filled with description after description of its glory. Time nor space nor human vocabulary permits us to attempt an explanation of its radiance.

HEAVEN IS A PLACE OF REST

So much of life on this planet is filled with exhaustion, mourning, struggles, and pressures of all kinds. But when we walk down heaven's golden streets, we will never see a hospital. There will be no more sickness. We will never see a counseling center. There will be no more depression or mental illness. We will never see a funeral home. There will be no more death there. We will never see a policeman in uniform or a police station. There is no crime there. There will be no courthouses on the square. There will be no lawsuits and no one seeking to cheat anyone else out of something that is rightfully theirs. We will never hear the shrill sound of an ambulance siren. There will be no more emergencies. We will never have to lock our homes or look behind us to see who is following us as we walk along. There will be no more fear. We will never see a handicapped parking place or a ramp for a wheelchair. There will be no nursing homes there for we will never grow old. Heaven is a place of rest.

There are several "no mores" in heaven. No more death. No more tears. No more mourning. No more crying. No more pain. No more farewells. No more separation. No more sorrow. No more sin. Whatever it is that may rob the joy out of life in this world will be gone—and gone forever. Heaven is a place of rest.

HEAVEN IS A PLACE OF RECOGNITION

We will know one another in heaven. In fact, the Bible says we will be known as we are known. When Peter, James, and John stood with Christ on the Mount of Transfiguration, Moses and Elijah appeared before them in their glorified forms and were readily recognized (Matthew 17). No one will have to introduce me to Paul or Peter or anyone else—and these heroes of the faith will know you and me. It is one thing for us to know the president of the United States, but it is quite something different for him to know us, to call us by name. In heaven we will know and be known.

Recently a NASA scientist speculated about the possibility of alien life on other planets. I have news for him. There is alien life on *our* planet. Those of us who are Christians are aliens in this world for "our citizenship is in heaven" (Philippians 3:20). We are citizens of another kingdom. We are simply passing through on our way home.

HEAVEN IS A PLACE OF REWARD

The Bible speaks repeatedly of certain crowns that will be given to believers as rewards in heaven. There is the crown of righteousness given to those who live godly lives and "all who have loved His appearing" (2 Timothy 4:8). There is also the incorruptible crown that will be presented to those who run the good race and finish strongly in the Christian faith (1 Corinthians 9:24–27 KJV). Next, there is the crown of life (Revelation 2:10). This crown is also referred to as the martyr's crown and is given to those who undergo severe trials and even death on Christ's behalf and in His service. There is also the crown of rejoicing, known as the soul winner's crown (1 Thessalonians 2:19–20). This reward is given to those men and women who are instrumental in leading other people to faith in Christ. Finally, there is the crown of glory given to faithful pastors and teachers who teach God's Word to others in truth and faithfulness (1 Peter 5:4).

These crowns are not to be worn by us as we strut up and down the streets of heaven. In one of the most humbling and beautiful scenes yet to unfold, we will take our crowns and cast them at Christ's feet. He alone is worthy to receive "power and riches and wisdom, and strength and honor and glory and blessing!" (Revelation 5:12).

Many seem to have the idea that heaven is a long way off. Not really. It is only one heartbeat away. James asked, "What is your life?" Then he answered his own question by indicating that life is really just a vapor. It appears for a little while and then vanishes away (James 4:14). For each of us, one of these days that old heart is going to stop. Then, in the wink of an eye, we will begin eternity . . . somewhere. Ten thousand years from today you will be alive . . . somewhere. Heaven awaits all who have come to God by faith alone in Christ. Jesus is the way, the only way, to the Father's house.

As you memorize this verse, meditate on the fact that your citizenship is in heaven. As the old spiritual attests, "This world is not my home, I'm just passing through." Who wouldn't want to live in a place like heaven . . . forever?

51 FAMOUS LAST WORDS

He who testifies to these things says,
"Surely I am coming quickly."
Amen. Even so, come, Lord Jesus!

REVELATION 22:20

The final words spoken by men and women are always intriguing. In this week's verse, we have the last promise of the Bible from the lips of Christ and the last prayer of the Bible from the lips of John. When, after His earthly mission, our Lord ascended back to the Father, two angels appeared to His followers, saying, "Men of Galilee, why do you stand gazing up into heaven? This same Jesus, who was taken up from you into heaven, will so come in like manner as you saw Him go into heaven" (Acts 1:11). Now, on the last page of the Bible, Jesus closes this Book of all books with the identical theme. This same Jesus promises, "Surely I am coming quickly." And each generation since the first century has been looking for "the Blessed Hope," His "glorious appearing" (Titus 2:13).

The Bible speaks of three major comings. First is the first coming of Christ, born of a virgin in the little obscure village of Bethlehem. He came and "dwelt among us" (John 1:14). For thirty-three years Jesus showed us a picture of true love. However, many did not recognize Him. They thought, at best, He was just another one of the prophets.

Next, there is the coming of the Holy Spirit foretold especially by the prophet Joel. This coming took place on the day of Pentecost when the Holy Spirit came to indwell believers, never to leave us, empowering us for service. In the old dispensation, the Holy Spirit came upon people, but when they became unfaithful, He left them. One of the saddest verses of Scripture is when the Bible reveals that the Holy Spirit "had departed" from Samson (Judges 16:20). King David, in his prayer of repentance in Psalm 51, prayed, "Do not take Your Holy Spirit from me" (v. 11). But today, in this dispensation of grace, no believer need ever pray that prayer. When we come to know Christ, the Holy Spirit comes to reside in us and promises that He will never leave us. As with the first coming of Christ, when the Holy Spirit came in this manner, many did not recognize Him. They accused those filled with the Spirit at Pentecost of being drunk (Acts 2:15).

The only major coming yet to be fulfilled is the return, the second coming of Jesus Christ. Just as surely as He came the first time, He is coming again. He is coming for His bride, the church. And when He reappears, all believers will recognize Him for who He is, our almighty King. The

Bible indicates that no one knows the day or the hour when our Lord will return (Mark 13:32). However, like with the other two major comings, there are signs and indications that this great event may be drawing near.

THE LAST PROMISE OF THE BIBLE

There are thousands of promises in the Bible. But the promise of Revelation 22:20, yet to be fulfilled, marks the climax of history. Jesus said, "Surely I am coming quickly." Are there any indications around us that this, the greatest event in human history, could happen soon? While no one can speculate as to an exact time, there are several events that will herald Jesus' return.

We are to watch for a *polluted pulpit*. The Bible says that one of the sure signs that Jesus' coming is near is a turning away from the truth in the churches. Paul said, "The time will come when they will not endure sound doctrine . . . and they will turn their ears away from the truth" (2 Timothy 4:3–4). We live in such a day: denominations are dying, and in many pulpits Jesus is no longer preached as "the way, the truth, and the life" (John 14:6).

We are to watch for a *particular place*. Before Christ returns, the Bible says, the little nation of Israel will once again become a major player on the world stage. God has promised that He will "bring back the captives of My people Israel" into their homeland (Amos 9:14). Our generation has seen the miracle of the rebirth of the state of Israel.

For the first time since the days of Nebuchadnezzar and the Babylonian captivity, the children of Israel are ruling their own country from their capitol of Jerusalem. After God's chosen people spent twenty-five hundred years in exile, I have witnessed this miracle with my own eyes in my generation.

We are to watch for a *peculiar people*. Moses, long ago, predicted that "the LORD will scatter you [the Jews] among the peoples" and that they would find no "resting place" in the world (Deuteronomy 4:27; 28:65). But Ezekiel talked of a day when God would "gather [His people] out of all the countries, and bring [them] back into your own land" (Ezekiel 36:24). While there is legitimate debate as to whether the present secular Zionist state is the biblical Israel to come, the fact remains that unusual things are happening among these "peculiar people," the Jews (Deuteronomy 26:18; Titus 2:14).

We are to watch for a *powerful politic*. The Bible indicates that, before the return of Christ, a powerful coalition of nations will emerge in Europe out of the ruins of the old Roman Empire. Daniel referred to this as "the ten horns" of the ancient Roman Empire (Daniel 7:15–25). From this new world order will emerge a one-world government with a common currency. This seems to be happening before our very eyes.

We are to watch for a *popular politician*. Shortly before the return of Christ, an electrifying leader will emerge on the world scene. He is called the Antichrist (1 John 2:18). This charismatic leader will promise a world of peace. He will promise to free the world of war and to bring about solutions to the world's economic and political problems. Much of the world will follow him.

We are to watch for a *pluralistic philosophy*. The Bible predicts that a new religion will emerge and seek to unite the world under one banner (2 Timothy 4:4). A new age of humanistic thought will seek to exalt man over Christ. Every time I see a New Age crystal hanging from a rear-view mirror, I want to join John in praying, "Even so, come, Lord Jesus!"

THE LAST PRAYER OF THE BIBLE

Having heard this amazing promise from His Savior's lips, John's first impulse is to burst out in prayer: "Even so, come, Lord Jesus!" (Revelation 22:20) Just five words. Often some of the most powerful prayers are the shortest ones. In this prayer John is anticipating the return of the Lord, which will usher in a new age of peace followed by the millennial reign of Christ on earth, followed by heaven, when time will be no more.

We will never know peace internationally until we have peace on a national level. This will never happen until we have peace on a state level. We will never see peace in our state until we have peace in our city. And peace will never come to our city until it comes to my street. This is impossible unless we have peace on my block. We will never have peace on my block until we have peace in my own home. And no true peace will exist in my home unless I have found peace in my own heart, and that comes only by my knowing the Prince of Peace Himself. Jesus is coming again to bring a kingdom of true and lasting peace among us. Join me in joining John and praying, "Even so, come, Lord Jesus!"

As you memorize this verse, meditate on this awesome event yet to come. And examine your life to make sure you are ready and will not be ashamed at His coming. "'Surely, I am coming quickly.' . . . Even so, come, Lord Jesus!"

52 THE FEAR FACTOR

Let us hear the conclusion of the whole matter:
Fear God and keep His commandments, for this is man's all.

❖❖❖❖❖❖❖❖❖❖❖❖❖❖

*W*e have come now to the end of this volume. It is fitting that at this point we hear the words of Solomon, the wisest man who ever lived, who, inspired by the Holy Spirit, said, "Let us hear the conclusion of the whole matter." Now this statement should make us perk up our ears. Solomon has promised to share "the conclusion of the whole matter." And here it is: *Fear God!* "Fear God and keep His commandments, for this is man's all."

But we live in what might be called a "no fear culture" today. We have raised a couple of generations with virtually no moral absolutes, so relativism rages in our society. Hence, young people live with no fear. There is even an apparel company that markets to this philosophy. Their caps and shirts carry a simple logo that says "No Fear." Unfortunately, instead of the church influencing the culture, the culture often influences the church. Thus, we awake to discover that the subject of the "fear of the Lord" has become a forgotten concept in many places of worship.

How long has it been since we have heard a sermon on—or given conscious expression ourselves to—the fear of the Lord? It is as though Isaiah was asking us and not simply his own culture, "Is there any among you who fears the Lord anymore?" (Isaiah 50:10).

A "WHY" QUESTION

Why are so many believers today living in a "no-fear culture" where the fear of the Lord is a forgotten topic? Could it be we have lost a sense of the holiness of our God? When Isaiah received the vision of the holiness of God, he said, "Woe is me" (Isaiah 6:5). When John saw the Lord in His glory, he said he fell down at his feet like a dead man (Revelation 1:17).

All through the Bible, there is one characteristic believers had in common: they lived in the fear of the Lord. All the Old Testament saints walked in the fear of God. Noah was "moved with godly fear" when he built the ark (Hebrews 11:7). The secret of the Proverbs 31 lady was that she "fears the LORD" (v. 30). The same is true in the gospels. The young virgin Mary sang in her song of praise, we call it the Magnificat, that God's "mercy is on those who fear Him" (Luke 1:50). Fear of the Lord is on most every page in Acts. At Pentecost we read that "fear came upon every soul, and many wonders and signs were done through the apostles" (Acts 2:43). Paul's epistles are replete with this same theme. To the Romans he said, "Stand by faith. Do not be haughty, but fear [God]" (Romans 11:20). In Ephesians 5:21, Paul stated, "[Submit] to one another in the fear of God." And, finally, in the last book of the Bible, as the final scene of heaven is revealed, John reported that a loud voice from the throne said, "Praise our God, all you His servants and those who fear Him, both small and great" (Revelation 19:5).

Thus, we are confronted with a "why" question. Why—when all those Old Testament saints, all those people throughout the Gospels, all those mentioned in Acts, all the instructions in the Epistles, and, finally, heaven itself—is this constant theme of all God's people a forgotten subject today? Have we lost a sense of the holiness of God?

A "WHAT" QUESTION

What does it mean to live in the fear of God? Does it mean we have to live in constant fright that if we say something or do something wrong, God will hit us with a big club of retribution? Nothing could be further from biblical reality. The most common Old Testament word for fear means "to stand before God with reverence and respect." The most common New Testament word for fear is closely akin to this. It speaks of a reverential awe that becomes the controlling motivation of our lives.

Long years ago, when I was a young believer, my pastor

taught me to walk in the fear of God. This fear wasn't any kind of worry that God was going to put His strong hand of discipline on me. The fear of God is not that He will put His hand *on* me, but the fear that He might take His hand *off* me. Fearing God is to live with the awareness that you do not want to do anything that might cause God to take His hand of blessing and anointing off you! Living with this conscious thought will make an incredible difference in our lifestyles as we walk in the fear of God.

A "HOW" QUESTION

Finally, how can we put a handle on biblical truth and begin living in the fear of the Lord ourselves? Where do we begin? We begin at the place where we begin everything in the Christian life: the Word of God. Solomon framed the subject best as God speaks through him directly to us: "If you receive my words, and treasure my commands . . . incline your ear to wisdom . . . apply your heart to understanding . . . cry out for discernment . . . lift up your voice for understanding . . . seek her as silver, and search for her as for hidden treasures; *then you will understand the fear of the Lord*" (Proverbs 2:1–5, emphasis added).

In your normal traffic pattern of devotional Bible reading, begin to circle the idea of the fear of the Lord every time you see it. You will be amazed how God will continue to bring it before you. Then you will begin walking in the fear of the Lord. It is a learned experience.

Yes, when the wisest man who ever lived, inspired by God's Spirit, says, "Let us hear the conclusion of the whole matter," it should make us really listen. This was Solomon's message: "Fear God and keep His commandments, for this is man's all."

As you memorize this verse, take your concordance and meditate on the references to the fear of God you will find there. And, along the way, remember that the fear of God is not the fear that He might put His hand of retribution *on* you, but the fear that He might take His hand of blessing and anointing *off* you. "Who among you who fears the LORD anymore?" (Isaiah 50:10).

THE GIFT OF ETERNAL LIFE

*I*t may be that, while you were reading this book, God's Spirit was leading you to put your faith and trust in Jesus Christ alone for eternal life. Heaven is God's free gift to you; it cannot be earned nor deserved. Yes, we are sinners and have all fallen short of God's perfect standard for our lives. He is a God of love and does not want to punish us for our sins, but He is also a God of justice and must punish sin.

This is where the Lord Jesus steps in. He is the infinite God-man who came to take our sins in His own body on the cross. Jesus became sin for us "that we might become the righteousness of God in Him" (2 Corinthians 5:21). However, it is not enough to simply know all these facts; we must individually transfer our trust from ourselves and our own human effort to Christ alone and put our faith in Him for our own personal salvation.

The Lord Jesus said, "Behold, I stand at the door and knock. If anyone hears My voice and opens the door, I will come in to him" (Revelation 3:20). If you would like to receive the free gift of eternal life through Jesus Christ, call on Him right now. He has promised that "whoever calls on the name of the LORD shall be saved" (Romans 10:13). The following is a suggested prayer:

Dear Lord Jesus,

I know I have sinned and do not deserve eternal life in and of myself. Thank You for dying on the cross for me. Please forgive me for my sin and come into my life right now. I turn to You and place all my trust in You for my eternal salvation. I accept Your free gift of eternal life and forgiveness right now. Thank You for coming into my life.

If this prayer is the desire of your heart, you can claim the promise Jesus made to those who believe in Him—"Most assuredly, I say to you, he who believes in Me has eternal life" (John 6:47).

You can now join millions of Christ's followers in saying, "You and You alone are the one and only Christ, the Savior of the world and the Lover of my soul." Tell someone what you have just done in receiving Christ as your own personal Savior!

MISSION:DIGNITY

*A*ll of the author's royalties and any proceeds from *The Joshua Code* go to the support of Mission:Dignity, a ministry of the Dallas-based Guide-Stone Financial Resources that enables thousands of retired ministers (and, in most cases, their widows) who are living below the poverty level, to live out their days with dignity and security. Many of them spent their pastoral ministry in small churches that were unable to provide adequately for their retirement. They also lived in church-owned parsonages and, upon their vocational retirement, had to vacate them as well. Mission:Dignity is a way of letting these good and godly servants know they are not forgotten and will be cared for in their declining years.

All of the expenses of this ministry are paid out of an endowment that has been raised for such, so that everyone who gives to Mission:Dignity can be assured that every cent of their gift goes to one of these precious saints in need.

For additional information regarding this ministry, please go to www.guidestone.org and click on the Mission:Dignity icon, or call toll-free at 1-888-98-GUIDE (1-888-984-8433).

OTHER BOOKS BY O. S. HAWKINS

When Revival Comes
(with Jack R. Taylor)

After Revival Comes

Clues to a Successful Life

Where Angels Fear to Tread

*Tracing the Rainbow
Through the Rain*

Revive Us Again

Unmasked!

*Jonah: Meeting the God
of the Second Chance*

In Sheep's Clothing

*Tearing Down Walls and
Building Bridges*

*Moral Earthquakes and
Secret Faults*

*Rebuilding: It's Never Too Late
for a New Beginning*

*Money Talks: But What
Is It Really Saying?*

*Shields of Brass or
Shields of Gold?*

Good News for Great Days

Drawing the Net

Culture Shock

High Calling, High Anxiety

The Question for Our Time

The Art of Connecting

*GuideStones: Ancient
Landmarks*

The Pastor's Primer

More Good News for Great Days

Getting Down to Brass Tacks

Antology

*The Pastor's Guide to Leading
and Living*

ABOUT THE AUTHOR

For more than twenty-five years, O. S. Hawkins served pastorates including the First Baptist Church in Fort Lauderdale, Florida, and the First Baptist Church in Dallas, Texas. A native of Fort Worth, he has three earned degrees (BA, MDiv, and DMin) and several honorary degrees. He is president of GuideStone Financial Resources, which serves 200,000 pastors, church staff members, missionaries, doctors, nurses, university professors, and other workers in various Christian organizations with their retirement and benefit service needs. He is the author of more than twenty-five books and preaches regularly at Bible conferences, evangelism conferences, and churches across the nation. He and his wife, Susie, have two married daughters and six grandchildren.